SAFE WITHIN YOUR LOVE

D1052894

REKINDLING
THE INNER FIRE

◆ ◆ ◆ ◆ ◆ ◆ ◆ ◆ ◆ ◆ ◆ ◆ ◆ ◆ ◆

SAFE WITHIN YOUR LOVE

◆

A 40-Day Journey
in the Company of

HANNAH W. SMITH

Devotional Readings Arranged
and Paraphrased by

David Hazard

BETHANY HOUSE PUBLISHERS

MINNEAPOLIS, MINNESOTA 55438
A Ministry of Bethany Fellowship, Inc.

All scripture quotations, unless indicated, are taken from the Holy Bible, New International Version. Copyright © 1973, 1978, 1984 International Bible Society. Used by permission of Zondervan Bible Publishers. All rights reserved.

Verses marked KJV are from the King James Version of the Bible.

Verses marked (TLB) are taken from the Living Bible ©1971 owned by assignment by Illinois regional Bank N.A. (as trustee). Used by permission of Tyndale House Publishers, Inc. Wheaton, IL 60189. All rights reserved.

Verses marked RSV are from the Revised Standard Version of the Bible, copyrighted 1946, 1952 ©1971, 1973 by the Division of Christian Education of the National Council of Churches of Christ in the USA, and used by permission.

Copyright © 1992
David Hazard
All Rights Reserved

Published by Bethany House Publishers
A Ministry of Bethany Fellowship, Inc.
6820 Auto Club Road, Minneapolis, Minnesota 55438

Printed in the United States of America

Library of Congress Cataloging-in-Publication Data

Smith, Hannah Whitall, 1832–1911
    Safe within your love / Hannah Whitall Smith ; arranged by David Hazard.
        p. cm. — (Rekindling the inner fire)

    1. Devotional exercises.   I. Hazard, David.
II. Title.
III. Series
BV4832.2.S5477   1992
242—dc20   92–25520
ISBN 1–55661–301–6   CIP

Foreword

Hannah Whitall (*White-all*) Smith once confessed that her spiritual writings were begun under extreme protest—as she put it, "at bayonet-point." She never intended to record the spiritual "secrets" that gave her comfort in the midst of desperate and painful circumstances. If her husband and a religious publisher had not hounded her for months, Hannah would never have penned the manuscript in 1875 that was destined to become a classic: *The Christian's Secret of a Happy Life*.

The monumental success of this book, which has brought spiritual life to many millions of Christians for generations, was as unexpected as the other turning points of Hannah's life— especially all the alarming losses that fanned the weak seed fire of her faith into a brilliant blaze that led other spiritual wanderers out of darkness toward the flame of God's love.

In the 1860s, Robert Pearsall Smith, Hannah's husband, rose to international acclaim as an evangelist. A few years before, Hannah had left the Quaker Meeting of Philadelphia she was born into in 1832, angering the Whitall family. Her

parents had always been liberal in allowing
Hannah to seek answers on her own—but then
they'd had no idea her questioning would lead
her out of their fold. Hannah's father threw her
out of his sitting room into the streets. Only
months of tearful pleadings by Hannah's mother
repaired the relationship.

Robert had likewise abandoned his Quaker
upbringing. He had quickly found fame as a
preacher of "the second blessing" of the Holy
Spirit. Hannah was unwillingly pulled into the
limelight after him.

For one thing, she was a young wife and
mother with small children in-tow. At a deeper
level, privately, she labored with guilt. She
distrusted the *razzle-dazzle* emotionalism that
seeped into some of the "spiritual revivals" then
taking place in the U.S. and Europe. She felt
there was too strong an emphasis on the
spiritual, and she sensed—before she could
articulate her feelings—that would backfire for
too many new believers. To her, all these
revelations, speaking in tongues, and personal
prophecies were a spiritual trap if converts were
not led to a deeper basis for their faith.

At that time, Hannah was in her early thirties,
and she'd already sought God down several
paths after leaving the Quaker Meeting. One
spiritual movement after another swept the
young nation. Independence was the spirit of the
age, and churches splintered off from one

another and spread across America like prairie flowers.

Hannah had turned away from the mystical pull of "Quietism" taught by their own Quakers. She viewed the fatalistic doctrine of presdestination spread by the strict Calvinists as a total misunderstanding of the ways of God. She watched the surges of "holiness" among Baptists and Plymouth Brethren lead to long lists of legalisms. And now Robert was caught up in these outburts of supernatural gifts (which predates the Azusa Street revivals by decades). There was even a rudimentary "faith movement," which insisted that Christian victory meant freedom from illness and poverty—that is, it promoted success in the *material* world as opposed to *spiritual* victory over the world-bound soul.

For Hannah, something solid and basic and true was missing in each of these popular movements of her day. Some were obviously too rigid and lifeless, while in others she saw that spirituality was bypassed in favor of carnival side-show. Robert, who was given to mood swings and favored with a gift of rhetoric, was rivetted to this "outpouring" of the Holy Spirit. What was it Hannah so deeply longed for? She could not put it into words, and this infuriated the high-strung Robert. Gradually she felt herself detached from most Christians and sadly isolated from her own husband.

Meanwhile, Robert and his friends pressured

Hannah to seek "the second blessing," by which they meant "the baptism in the Holy Ghost." For weeks, on her knees, Hannah tried. Nothing supernatural came of it. Robert was embarrassed by Hannah and privately told her she was nothing but "a dry stick" emotionally.

And yet. . .

It was true that Robert's charismas beamed from pulpits across the land. But it was to "dull" Hannah that Robert and many of his individual followers secretly turned one by one when their supernatural experiences began to dim. Later, other Christian "friends" would blame Hannah for not "praying in faith" when their five-year-old daughter died of scarlet fever. But Hannah saw this brand of "faith" as heresy—she viewed it as "faith in faith," a counterfeit of the deep true knowing of God that she hungered for. *I hunger for.*

As Hannah would later write, in the plain-spoken manner that characterizes all her works, mystical revelations and supernatural answers to prayer are wonderful "when you can manage to have them." But, she observed, "you cannot always drum one up at the moment you need it."

All the condemnation that Robert and others heaped on Hannah drove her from one spiritual "in" circle after another. To her, their intense super-spirituality seemed only a big emotional splash, followed by months of little experiential ripples petering away to near nothing. But where was she to turn? She could not return to flat-footed fundamentalism. For as she wrote later,

10

"There is a great deal of longing and hoping among this generation of Christians"—by which she meant mental assent to the truths in the Bible—"but there is not much of *knowing* God himself."

In a way, Hannah was pushed out of the various societies of the faithful and forced on a lonely way toward the arms of her heavenly Father.

The very words of the Bible became illuminated to her. She had no tolerance for doctrines, or for rules, or for the mere history of the Bible stories. It was as if the vellum pages of scripture were a thin veil that she was able to look *through* and see a glimpse of her Father in heaven. And here were the few solid, basic truths on which she came to stake her life and her sacred faith.

As if she'd had one of those dramatic revelations, Hannah *saw* the goodness of God, took in the wonder of His Fatherhood, understood that He is magnificent enough to turn all the evil that arrows into the lives of His children into utter good if we but place all circumstances into His tender hands. Truths about the character of God himself settled like unshakable stones at the bottom of her soul.

Robert was publishing a newsletter for the growing throngs of supporters across the nation and overseas. He beseiged Hannah until she gave in and wrote a series of articles about these spiritual "secrets" she was learning—and she was learning them in the nick of time.

Everything Hannah claimed she had discovered about the Christian's secret of a happy life was about to be tested in destruction and fire.

In the summer of 1875, Robert began a months-long tour of churches throughout England and much of Europe. He'd been pressing Hannah to write a few articles for the newsletter he mailed to ardent followers—and these short pieces had been collected by the Fleming H. Ravell Company in New Jersey as the basis for a book. On the ship bound for England, Hannah was worn down by seasickness and by Robert's pressure, and she consented to finish the manuscript. This she mailed back to the States when they arrived in London.

Now, the great irony. *The Christian's Secret of a Happy Life* rapidly became a bestseller back in the United States, raising its still-absent author to celebrity status. The publisher's telegrams were ecstatic. And during the European tour, Robert was found in the bedroom of a female admirer. It's likely that he was only offering "spiritual counsel," as he insisted. But in those days even the sniff of a scandal brought intense disgrace.

Church doors suddenly slammed in thier faces. Friends abandoned them. Cabled messages denounced Robert back home long before he could return to defend himself.

And so Robert's star set at the very moment Hannah's began to rise. He returned to America in disgrace and suffered a nervous breakdown.

She returned to an outcry for more of her writings.

At the urging of a few friends, Robert made one halfhearted attempt to regain his footing in the American churches. But now he was an embittered man, given more to moods and depressions than ever before. Eventually, his bleak emotions became a permanent state of doubt. He gave up preaching, and his faith ebbed out.

Once a brilliant superstar of the pulpit, Robert now sulked around the house, muttering dark agnosticisms. Or else he went out on long walks that led him, as Hannah was soon to discover, to the parlors of several "lady friends."

Hannah had already lost another child, her most devout one, Frank, to scarlet fever when he was just eighteen. Now Robert weedeled around their remaining three children—Logan, Alys, and Mary—attempting to win them over to his side of unbelief. The war in spirit had now invaded Hannah's own once-peaceful, once-Christian home life.

From this time on, you might view Hannah's life as a string of disasters: One daughter would abandon her husband and run off with an artist; another daughter married one of the most outspoken atheists, Bertrand Russell; Robert continued to visit his mistresses. Hannah herself was plagued with a burning arthritis. And, like so many great souls of the church before her, she would also be openly denounced, and on one

13

occasion even had a wet towel slapped across her face as she spoke to a crowd. But Hannah did not view these things, painful as they were, as defeats.

One by one, it seems that God removed from Hannah all possible attachments to the world. And still the words of Scripture were alight with "sanctified common sense." In response to all her "losses," Hannah attached herself more firmly than ever to Him whom she saw as utterly good and unselfish in all His ways. She would write:

> God alone is unchangeable. What we call spiritual blessings are full of the element of change. The prayer that is answered today may seem to be unanswered tomorrow. The promises once so gloriously fulfilled may cease to have any apparent fulfillment. . . . But when all else is gone, God is left and nothing changes Him . . . the soul that finds its joy in Him alone will suffer no wavering. (*Everyday Religion*)

Hannah wrote other books: *The Unselfishness of God and How I Discovered It* and *Everyday Religion* among them. Then she retired to Oxford, England, where she affirmed a few years before her death in 1911 these closing words to her book *God of All Comfort*: "Nothing can separate you from [God's] love, absolutely nothing. . . . God is enough for time, and God is enough for eternity. *God is enough!*"

In all of Hannah's writing, as in her life, nothing stands out so brightly as the light of God the Father as she discovered it—in all His sweet goodness, and totally unselfish. Her conviction that God was purely loving in all His ways was the only great "spiritual secret" she would ever cling to, to the end. On a spring day in 1911, she was "gathered" to God, as the Quakers put it.

Hannah, who longed to know God above all else, has left us with an urgent question: Who can hold back from giving oneself totally to a Father who loves us so dearly?

Work on this volume of the "Rekindling" devotional series was greatly helped by two generous friends. Barbara Halpern, Hannah's direct descendant, allowed me permission to quote from unpublished correspondence. And Marie Henry, who supplied several out-of-print books, gave invaluable insights into Hannah's private life through her wonderful biography of Hannah.

As with the other works in this series, the arrangement, phrasing and editing are mine, as are the prayers that close the day's entry. Since Hannah preferred the customary Quaker "thees" and "thous" in personal correspondence, they are intact.

May Hannah's life—and her intense conviction that God is first and always on our side, turning all pain and evil to our good—set in you a new burning to know God. And may you find for yourself that God longs to keep you, no matter your circumstances, safe within His love.

David Hazard
July 1992

Contents

SAFE
WITHIN
YOUR
LOVE

1
Turning for Home

Lord, you have been our dwelling place throughout
all generations.

Psalm 90:1

Jesus said, "Before long, the world will not see me
anymore, but you will see me. . . . He who loves me
will be loved by my Father, and I too will love him
. . . we will come to him and make our home with
him."

John 14:19, 21, 23

Our "dwelling place" is not merely a place
where we visit. It is our home. All the interests of
our earthly lives center in our home; we do all we
can to make it attractive and comfortable. But our
souls need a comfortable dwelling place even
more than our bodies. . . .

Where the soul is full of peace and joy,
outward surroundings and circumstances are of
comparatively little account. It is of vital

importance, then, that we should determine where our souls are living. The Lord declares that He has been our dwelling place throughout all ages, but the question is: Are you and I living in our true home?

The psalmist says of the children of Israel that they "wandered in desert wastelands, finding no way to a city where they could settle. They were hungry and thirsty, and their lives ebbed away" (Psalm 107:4–5).

I am afraid there are many wandering souls in the church of Christ, whom this description of the wandering Israelites would exactly fit. All their Christian lives they have felt themselves wandering in a spiritual wilderness, and have found no "city" to dwell in. Hungry and thirsty, they feel their lives ebbing away.

And yet all the while the dwelling place of God has been standing wide open, inviting them to come in and take up their rest and peace there forever! Our Lord Jesus himself urges this invitation upon us. "Abide in me," He says, "and I in you" (John 15:4, KJV). The truth is, our souls are made for God. He is our natural home, and we can never be at rest anywhere else.

How shall we describe this divine dwelling place? David describes it when he says: "The Lord is my rock, my fortress, and my deliverer" (Psalm 18:2).

When we are told that God, who is our dwelling place, is also our fortress, it can only mean one thing, and that is, that if we will but live in our dwelling place, we shall be perfectly safe and secure from every assault of every possible enemy that can attack us. . . .

"In the shelter of your presence you hide [me] from the intrigues of men; in your dwelling you keep [me] safe from accusing tongues" (Psalm 31:20). The "shelter of His presence" is safer than a thousand Gibraltars!

I do not mean that no trials will come. They may come in abundance. But they cannot penetrate into the sanctuary of the soul when it is settled in God, and we may dwell in perfect peace. . . .

GOD OF ALL COMFORT: Ch. 8

My Father, it's true that I wander in some desert places trying to find for myself a place of safety and strength. Today, I hear you calling me to continue my soul's journey home to you.

I set my face toward your welcoming light, toward the banquet that is spread for me in your love. I come now, to meet you in the secret holy place of your Spirit. . . .

2
We Know. . . .

. . . everyone born of God overcomes the world. . . .
Who is it that overcomes the world? Only he who
believes that Jesus is the Son of God.
Anyone who does not believe God has made him out to
be a liar. . . .
I write these things to you who believe in the name of
the Son of God so that you may know. . . .

1 John 5:4–5, 10, 13, *emphasis added*

One of the most commonsense principles in
the physical realm of everyday life is this: We
need to have clear knowledge of both our earthly
position—so we are not constantly getting lost—
and our earthly possessions—so we know the
resources at our disposal.

Nothing is plainer in the Bible than that we
are meant to have this sure knowledge in our
spiritual life as well. Uncertainty hinders our
spiritual progress and destroys comfort and
peace. Yet it has somehow become the fashion
among Christians to encourage uncertainty in the

spiritual life, and to accept uncertainty as a sign of healthy spirituality.

There is a great deal of longing and hope among Christians, but there is not much knowing. And yet the Bible was written for the purpose of making us know. . . . And the Holy Spirit is given to us Christians not to make us have longings and hopes only, but to enable us to "know the things that are freely given to us of God" (1 Corinthians 2:12, KJV).

Doubts and uncertainties about spiritual things belong to and come from the ungodly spirit of this world. Steadfast knowledge belongs to and comes from the Spirit of God. As long as we fail to say "I know" in regard to spiritual things, we are allowing the spirit of this world to rule instead of the Spirit of God.

In the Bible it is always taken for granted that we know. . . .

"I do not write to you because you do not know the truth, but because you do know it and because no lie comes from the truth" (1 John 2:21). We know also that the Son of God has come and has given us understanding (1 John 5:20). We know that in all things God works for the good of those who love him, who have been called according to his purpose (Romans 8:28). The Bible is full of declarations like these. But how would they sound if we should substitute in them all the word *hope* for the word *know*? Never anywhere in the whole Bible are we given the slightest intimation that God's children are to be anything but perfectly sure of our relationship to Him as children, and of His relationship to us as Father.

We are not commanded to be followers of God in order to become His children, but because we know we *are* His children.

A man cannot act like a king unless he knows that he is a king. Similarly, we cannot act like the sons of God unless we know that we are His sons. This knowledge, of our position and standing, is the essential foundation of everything else in the Christian life.

EVERYDAY RELIGION: Ch. 1

My Father, I will no longer make you out to be a liar. I will take my eyes off "bad circumstances" and look with the spiritual eyes and with belief . . . looking to the higher, greater spiritual work you are doing in me in every situation.

Today, I will not say, doubtfully, "I hope." Instead, I will begin to say, "I know."

3
Hidden With Christ

. . . set your hearts on things above, where Christ is seated at the right hand of God. Set your minds on things above, not on earthly things. For you died, and your life is now hidden with Christ in God. . . .
Christ . . . is your life. . . .

Colossians 3:1–4

*T*he "higher" Christian life . . . is the only true Christian life. To my own mind it is best described in the words "the life hidden with Christ in God."

I consider it as a settled point that the Scriptures do set before the believer in the Lord Jesus a life of abiding rest and continual victory, which is far beyond the ordinary run of Christian experience.

The chief characteristics of "the life hidden with Christ" in God are these: entire surrender to the Lord, and a perfect trust in Him. This will result in victory . . . and inward rest of soul. It differs from the lower range of Christian experience in that it causes us to let the Lord carry our burdens and manage our affairs for us, instead of trying to do most of it ourselves.

Most of us, however, are like the man who was toiling along a road, bending under a heavy burden. Soon a wagon overtook him and the driver kindly offered to help him on his journey. The man happily accepted the offer, but when he was seated on the wagon he continued to bend under his burden, which he still kept on his shoulders.

"Why don't you lay down your burden?" asked the kindhearted driver.

"Oh no!" replied the man. "I feel it's almost too much to ask you to carry me. I couldn't think of letting you carry my burden too."

And so Christians—those who have given themselves to the care and keeping of the Lord Jesus—still continue to bend beneath the weight of their burdens, and often go weary and heavy-laden throughout the whole length of their journey.

When I speak of burdens, I mean everything that troubles us, whether spiritual or temporal.

I mean, first of all, ourselves. The greatest burden we have to carry in life is *self*. The most difficult thing we have to manage is *self*. Our own daily living—our moods and feelings, our special weaknesses and temptations, our peculiar

temperaments and inward affairs of every kind—
these are the things that disturb and worry us
more than anything else, and that frequently lead
us back into bondage and darkness.

In laying off your burdens, therefore, the first
one you must get rid of is yourself. You must
hand yourself—with your temptations, your
temperament, your moods and feelings, every
inward and outward experience, the whole of
your life—into the care of your God. Daily,
minute by minute, determine to leave it there.

God made you and therefore understands you
and knows how to manage you. You must trust
Him to do it.

THE CHRISTIAN'S SECRET OF A HAPPY LIFE: Ch. 3

My Father, *contained in this one small
word—me—are so many heavy burdens.*

*Now I see it: If I am still trying to manage any
great weight alone—an everyday problem, or a
spiritual one—then I will always stumble and fall on
my journey in you.*

*Today, I lay in your hands the greatest thing that
weighs me down . . . which is my self.*

4

The Unfinished Name of God

*M*oses said to God, "Suppose I go to the Israelites
and say to them, 'The God of your fathers has sent me
to you,' and they ask me, 'What is his name?' Then
what shall I tell them?"

Exodus 3:13

I will sing praise to your name, O Most High. . . .
Those who know your name will trust in you, for you,
Lord, have never forsaken those who seek you.

Psalm 9:2, 10

*T*he greatest question of all ages, and of
every human heart, is expressed here: "What is
the name of God?"

And the whole fate of every one of us hangs
on the answer to it. . . . Everything in the
universe depends upon the sort of creator who
has brought it into existence, right down to the

33

everyday welfare of the human beings who have been placed there.

If the God who created us is a good God, then everything must of necessity be all right for us. A good God cannot ordain any but good things. But if He is a bad God, or careless, or unkind. . . .

Each of us who say we are in Christ must answer this first great question for ourselves. What is God's name—or what is His character, what sort of God is He?

God answered Moses' question this way—He said, "I AM WHO I AM . . . say to the Israelites, I AM has sent me to you. . . . This is my name forever . . ." (Exodus 3:14–15).

In the Gospel of John, Jesus adopts this name *I am* as His own. When the Jews were questioning Him as to His authority, Jesus said to them, "Before Abraham was, I am" (John 8:58, KJV). And in the Book of Revelation, He again declares, "I am the Alpha and the Omega . . . who is, and who was, and who is to come, the Almighty" (1:8).

These words—I am—express eternity, and One who exists without being subject to change. And this is the very first trait necessary in a God we can depend upon, for we cannot depend upon a God who is changeable.

But what does this name *I am* imply? We must ask, "I am what?" What does the I am include?

I'm now convinced it includes everything the human heart longs for and needs. For this name of God is an unfinished name—it seems to me that it is like a blank check, signed by a very wealthy friend, and given to us to be filled in with whatever sum we wish.

Every attribute of God, every revelation of His character, every proof of His undying love, every declaration of His watchful care, every assurance that all His purposes for us are wrapped in His tender mercy, every possible manifestation of His lovingkindness—all are included in God's unfinished name, and waiting for us to draw upon.

God tells us, through all the pages of His Book, what He is, and what His name means for us:

"I am all that my people need or desire" (Psalm 145:16; Ephesians 3:20).

"I am your strength" (Psalm 18; 1 Timothy 1:12).

"I am your wisdom" (Proverbs 2:6; 1 Corinthians 1:30).

"I am your righteousness" (Isaiah 45; Romans 10:4).

"I am your peace" (Isaiah 9:6; Romans 1:7).

"I am your salvation" (Psalm 62:2; 2 Timothy 2:10).

"I am your life" (Psalm 27:1; John 1).

This apparently unfinished name, therefore, is the most comforting name the heart of man could devise. The very name of our God allows us to add to it, without any limitation, whatever it is we need.

GOD OF ALL COMFORT: Ch. 2

My comforting Father, *I thank you that you are not brutal when you open my eyes to all that I am not.*

Only draw my eyes away and up to all that you are, so that I can become more whole and complete today . . . in you.

5
Spiritual Worship

Do not yield your members to sin as instruments of wickedness, but yield yourselves to God as men who have been brought from death to life, and your members as instruments of righteousness.
For sin shall not be your master, because you are not under law, but under grace.

Romans 6:13, RSV; v.14, NIV

To *yield* means simply to "sign over" something to the care and keeping of another. To yield ourselves to the Lord, therefore, is to sign ourselves over to Him—it means to give Him entire possession and control of all that we are and all that we own. We abandon ourselves to His care, and take our hands off ourselves.

The word *consecration* is often used by Christians to express this yielding. I hardly think it is a good word to use. With many of us, consecrating ourselves comes to mean that we are doing something self-sacrificing, something very good and grand. And so it becomes a kind of subtle self-glorification.

Yielding conveys a far more humbling idea. It implies helplessness and weakness, and glorifies another rather than ourselves.

If I were lost in a wild and lonely forest and a skilled guide should come to my rescue, I would not consecrate myself to that guide. But I would yield my care and guidance to him.

This is more than mere words. To *consecrate* is an Old Testament idea, and belongs to the old covenant of works. A form of the word is used forty times in the Old Testament, and only twice in the New—and both times it refers to Christ! (Hebrews 7:28; 10:20, KJV).

The New Testament idea of yielding or surrender is set forth plainly by the Apostle Paul: "I urge you, brothers, in view of God's mercy, to offer your bodies as living sacrifices, holy and pleasing to God—this is your spiritual act of worship" (Romans 12:1).

We are to present ourselves—offer ourselves, hand ourselves over. To do with ourselves as we would do with the money we entrust to the bank—that is, submit ourselves to the care, keeping and use of God. It is not the dark idea of physical sacrifice, or the sense of a great cross we must carry achingly on our shoulders. It is the wonderful sense of a burden laid down, of giving up the control and keeping of ourselves to the Lord.

It certainly is profound common sense to place our treatment for a physical illness into the hands of a skillful physician. And it is the most profound common sense of all to put our poor, weak, foolish and helpless selves into the care and keeping of the God who made us, who loves us, and who alone can care for us. When we yield to God, it means we then belong to God, and that we now have all His infinite power and infinite love at work on our side!

What I am inviting you to do is this: Yield yourself to Him. Take advantage of this amazing privilege that human words cannot even express. . . .

Regardless of circumstances or of consequences . . . yield.

EVERYDAY RELIGION: Ch. 4

My Father, *I know that when I yield myself to you, you will not forget me, will not waste my life . . . because you value me.*

Invest me today, Father, where you will.

6
Ours in Christ

All I have is yours. . . .

John 17:10

The Lord is my shepherd, I shall lack nothing. . . .
You prepare a table before me. . . . You anoint my
head with oil; my cup overflows.

Psalm 23:1, 5

Recognition is my great word just now. All
things are provided and are even already given;
only recognize that you have them. This is
Scripture, and it is divine common sense.

"All things are yours" (I Corinthians 3:21).

"He hath blessed us with all spiritual blessings
in Christ" (Ephesians 1:3, KJV).

"Seek and you will find" (Matthew 7:7–8).

Of course—because it is all here already, and
all is ours! Oh, what we have missed all these
years from not having had eyes that could see. I
have hungered so for things that all the time I

41

possessed, if I had only known it.

Somehow my two summers out in the wilds of nature, with no meetings and no religious influences—only God and His works— have been more to me in my interior life than any other thing I have ever known. They have brought me face-to-face with God, and I have seen Him.

Not in a vision, as so many think is the only way of seeing; but as one sees the truth—that is, comprehends it. And in this type of spiritual sight, I have found what I never expected to find—more emotional joy than I have ever known before.

The fact is, our God is so wonderfully good, and lovely, and blessed in every way that the mere fact of belonging to Him is enough for an untellable fullness of joy!

UNPUBLISHED LETTER: November 24, 1881

My Father, so often I focus on what I lack. And I complain.

Open my eyes to the bounty of blessings you have given me. Most especially, open my eyes to you. . . .

7
God Is Not Lost— We Are

*This is what the Sovereign Lord says, "I myself will
search for my sheep and look after them. . . . I will
rescue them from all the places where they were
scattered on a day of cloud and darkness. . . . I will
tend them in a good pasture. . . . there they will lie
down in good grazing land. . . . I will search for the
lost and bring back the strays. I will bind up the
injured and strengthen the weak. . . ."*

*Jesus told them . . . "Suppose one of you has a
hundred sheep and loses one of them. Does he not
leave the ninety-nine in the open country and go after
the lost sheep until he finds it? And when he finds it,
he joyfully puts it on his shoulders and goes home."*

Luke 15:3–5

Christ came to seek and save us, because as
men and women on our own we are lost.

God's part is always to run after us . . . but in
our foolishness we do not understand it this way.

We think the Lord is the one who is lost and must be found, and that it is our part to find Him.

The very expressions we often use betray us. We tell sinners to "seek the Lord." We talk about having "found the Lord."

A too-zealous Christian worker asked a happy little girl, "Have you found the Savior?"

Innocently, and with a look of amazement, the little child replied, "I didn't know He was lost!"

It is our ignorance of God that causes us to think of Him in wrong and confused ways.

You may say, "But how am I to get to know Him? Other people seem to have special, inward revelations that make them know Him. But I never do. And no matter how much I pray, spiritual things and the real presence of God seem distant and dark to me."

For most of us, our trouble is that we have the wrong idea of what knowing God is all about—or at least the kind of knowing I mean. For I don't mean any mystical, interior revelations of any kind. Such revelations are wonderful, when you can have them—but they are not always at our command, and they are often shaky and uncertain.

The kind of knowing I mean is this: the plain matter-of-fact certainty that comes when you and I decide we will believe what is written in the Bible about God.

I mean, to say it in practical terms, that when

I read in the Bible, "God is love" (1 John 4:16), I am to believe it . . . whether I have any inward revelation of it or not. For it is vitally important to understand that the Bible is a statement, not of theories but of facts . . . they are only in the Bible because they are true.

It was a great discovery to me when I grasped this idea.

Inward revelations we cannot call to ourselves whenever we will, but anyone in possession of his senses can believe the thing that is written.

To some, this may seem a very dry and bare way to start. But if you steadfastly persevere, it will result in very blessed inward revelations. And sooner or later it will lead us out into such a knowledge of God that will transform our lives.

This kind of knowing brings us convictions. And to my mind convictions are far superior to any inward revelations, delightful as these are.

GOD OF ALL COMFORT: Ch. 1

My Father . . . Good Shepherd! I see that my thinking is all wrong and that you were never lost . . . and I am the one who wanders.

Find me, Father! Walk all the tangled pathways of my heart that remain. Hear me when I call, when the thorns catch and cut. And carry me on your shoulders . . . home.

8
Things That Hinder . . . Today

. . . let us throw off everything that hinders and the sin that so easily entangles, and let us run with perseverance the race marked out for us. Let us fix our eyes on Jesus, the author and perfecter of our faith. . . .

———

Hebrews 12:1–2

*D*on't worry about anything; instead, pray about everything; tell God your needs and don't forget to thank him for His answers. If you do this you will experience God's peace, which is far more wonderful than the human mind can understand. His peace will keep your thoughts and your hearts quiet and at rest as you trust. . . .

———

Philippians 4:6–7, TLB

*T*he Christian may freely "throw off" every burden—of health, reputation, Christian work, house and possessions, concerns for children, business, employees. In short, everything that causes concern, whether inward or outward in nature.

For many people, it is generally much less difficult to commit the keeping of the future to the Lord than it is to commit the present. Many recognize that we are helpless in regard to the future, but we feel as if the present were in our own hands and must be carried on our own shoulders.

I knew a Christian woman who had a great "burden" in her life. Her concern caused her to lose sleep and her appetite, and soon her health was in danger of breaking down. . . . She recognized, however, that she could in no way alter her circumstances and therefore resolved to try a new plan.

She took her circumstances to the Lord. She handed them over to His management. Then she simply believed that from that very moment He took them. She decided to leave all responsibility, and her mental worrying and anxious feelings, with Him, too.

Of course, all of these tormenting things tried time and again to return. And each time, she took them back to the Lord. As a result— although the outward circumstances did not change—her soul began to experience perfect peace in the midst of trouble.

She rejoiced at having entered into such a

practical secret of the spiritual life. And from that time, she set this as her goal: Never to carry her own burdens nor to manage her own affairs, but to hand them over as fast as they arose to the divine Burden-bearer.

This same secret, which was so effective in dealing with outward circumstances, she began to apply to her inward life—because, in fact, her moods and emotions were even more utterly unmanageable. So she abandoned her whole self to the Lord, all that she was, as well as all that she had. She believed that He took what she committed to Him, and determined that she would cease fretting and worrying.

And so she found a new light dawning within, and felt flooded with the gladness that comes when we know we belong to God. By applying this simple secret, she discovered that it is possible to obey God's loving commandment, contained in the words: "Do not worry about anything."

The inevitable result is that the peace of God, which comes when we step beyond our understanding and into trust, will take hold of our heart and mind.

THE CHRISTIAN'S SECRET OF A HAPPY LIFE: Ch. 2

My Father, friends have failed me at times . . . and I have failed them. . . . Forgive me for *thinking that you are weak like us.*

You promise to be loyal, and never to fail me . . . and I can trust you with the thing that weighs on me today.

9
God Is a Fact

*[God] has brought you back [to himself] as his
friends . . . Christ has brought you into the very
presence of God, and you are standing there before
him with nothing left against you—nothing left that
he could even chide you for; the only condition is that
you fully believe the truth, standing in it steadfast and
firm, strong in the Lord, convinced . . . that Jesus
died for you, and never shifting from trusting him to
save you. This is the wonderful news. . . .*

Colossians 1:22–23

*. . . anyone who comes to [God] must believe that he
exists. . . .*

Hebrews 11:6

I was twenty-six years old and had just lost a
precious little daughter five years old. My heart
was aching with sorrow I could not endure. . . .
No matter on which side I turned there was no
ray of light.

How it first commenced I have no idea, but somehow, standing in the dark, cold prison-depths of my pain, the inner "eyes of my soul" seemed to open slowly. I saw, as in a sudden blaze of light that, after all else is said and done, God is a fact.

I saw that He is the solid bedrock of all facts.

From then on the only thing I could do was to find out all about Him. I did not have any pious feeling, which I had been looking for, but now I had conviction—just the kind of conviction that comes when a mathematical problem has been solved. You do not *feel* that such a problem is solved, you *know* it, and there can be no further question.

In this way, God was making himself "visible" and "present" to me, as a God who actually exists.

Someone had remarked once in my hearing that the book of Romans contained the clearest and fullest statements of the Christian belief to be found in the whole Bible, and I set myself to read it. . . . Baldly stated, [the plan for salvation] described there is as follows:

We were all sinners, and therefore all deserved punishment. But Christ took our sins upon himself and bore the punishment in our stead. Therefore, any possible anger of God was satisfied, and He is now willing to forgive us and let us go free.

Nothing could be more plain or simple! A

child could understand it: Why hadn't I? The act that accomplished our forgiveness and freedom was all outside of myself—done by someone else for me, with nothing I could add to it. I no longer needed to scrape and search for every sin lurking within me, nor to rake up grand spiritual feelings to convince myself I was now right with God.

Christ has made things right. I had nothing to do but accept it all as a free gift from Him. Moreover, I understood that a Father-God who would arrange such a simple plan as this was a God I could easily understand, a God I could approach without fear or timidity, and I began to think, *It must be true!*

THE UNSELFISHNESS OF GOD: Ch. 18

My Father, from all eternity,
I am so centered on myself and, like a little child with his hands over his eyes, I suppose that because I cannot see you, you cannot see me. Forgive my childishness.

Now . . . in this moment . . . I will let go of my blind supposings . . . and in spirit I will hold in my hands the fact of you.

10
Holy Common Sense

*W*ait for the Lord and keep his way. . . .

———

Psalm 37:34

. . . the Counselor, the Holy Spirit, whom the Father
will send in my name, will teach you all things. . . .

———

John 14:26

*I*t is essential to remember, in the spiritual
life, that the Bible is a book of solid principles,
not some book of disjointed truisms.

Too often, Christians fall into the trap of using
isolated texts to sanction things, which the
principles of Scripture totally oppose. I believe all
fanaticism comes in this way: An isolated text is
so impressed upon a man or woman's mind that
they feel compelled to obey it, no matter into
what wrong or hurtful behavior it may lead. Thus
they go off, violating the spiritual principles of

Scripture, while telling everyone they are obeying it.

Remember: In Luke 4, the enemy used isolated texts to support his temptations; Jesus repelled his attack by declaring the correct spiritual principles.

Therefore, if you search the Bible and do not find the spiritual principle that will settle your special point of difficulty, you must seek guidance in other ways.

God will surely voice himself to you as He has promised: either by an inner conviction that directs you or by circumstances that can only have come about by the arrangement of "providence" or by a clear inner "message." And before you act on any of these, you must see whether it is in accordance with Scripture . . . and whether, as we Quakers say, the "way opens" for you.

If any one of these tests fails, it is not safe to proceed. You must wait in quiet trust, until the Lord shows you clearly the point of harmony. And He surely will, sooner or later.

What I am telling you is this: It is not enough that our "leadings" should be tested by the teaching of Scripture. . . . They must be tested as well by our own spiritually enlightened judgment—or what is familiarly called common sense.

So far as I can see, the Scriptures everywhere make it an essential thing for the children of God in their journey through this world, to use all the faculties that have been given to them.

Some of you may object, saying, "I thought that we were not to depend on our human understanding in spiritual things!" That is true enough. We are not to depend on our unenlightened human understanding—but we are to involve our human judgment and common sense enlightened by the Spirit of God. That is, God will speak to us through all the faculties He himself has given us, and not independently of them.

And so, just as we are to use our physical eyes in our outward life—and no matter how full of "faith" we may be—God wants us to use our spiritual eyes of understanding in our interior walk with Him.

THE CHRISTIAN'S SECRET OF A HAPPY LIFE: Ch. 8

My Father, I will not crash on ahead today in any matter where I've felt turmoil. I will wait for you . . .

. . . trusting that your Spirit will show me the right path . . . at the right time . . . and give me the common sense to know how.

11
Hungering in the Wilderness

Come . . . you who have no money, come, buy and eat! . . . Why spend money on what is not bread, and your labor on what does not satisfy? Listen, listen to me, and eat what is good, and your soul will delight in the richest of fare.

Isaiah 55:1–2

Give us this day our daily bread. . . .

Matthew 6:11, KJV

Good common sense must tell us that our souls need daily food just as much as our bodies. Unless Christianity contains this necessary food for our daily lives, it is a grievous failure. But God does provide.

"Give us this day our daily bread" is a prayer that includes the cry of the soul as well as the body. For our part, it is important that we choose

59

the right sort of spiritual food on which to feed.

If parents allowed it, some children would eat much candy, cookies, and other sweets all day long and, as a result, would be listless and irritable and eventually become ill. Doesn't reason tell us that, when we feed our souls upon a diet of worldly novels, or gossip, or draw our only inner refreshment from frivolities of every kind, then we will necessarily suffer with a spiritual sluggishness and fatigue? That we will be unable to take in and "digest" spiritual meat? That if we take in darkness, we will feel goodness and spiritual vitality drain away? That we will soon be overtaken by a moral paralysis, so that we are unable to respond to evil with godliness?

"The children of Israel lusted exceedingly in the wilderness, and tempted God in the desert. And he gave them their request; but sent leanness into their soul" (Psalm 106:14–15, KJV).

Leanness of soul arises far more often than we think from the indigestible nature of the spiritual food we have been feeding upon. We are not satisfied to eat the food God has provided for us, and we hunger for the "flesh pots of Egypt" (Exodus 16:3, KJV).

We must first understand our dissatisfaction.

Perhaps you do not like the circumstances and surroundings in which you find yourself—or your preacher, or your work, or members of your own family. You think all the time that you could be a better Christian if only your circumstances were different—if you could attend a different church, or move into a different neighborhood, or engage in a different sort of work. Your human soul "loathes the light food" that God is providing. You question, as the Israelites did, whether God is really able to provide the spiritual food necessary to sustain you in your particular wilderness, where He seems to have appointed your "dwelling place."

"They spoke against God, saying, 'Can God spread a table in the desert?' . . . When the Lord heard them, he was very angry . . . and his wrath rose . . ." (Psalm 78:19, 21).

The "wrath of God" is only another name for the inevitable results of our own bad actions. God's wrath is never (as human wrath generally is) an arbitrary condition of His mind, resulting from His displeasure at being crossed. It is simply the necessary result that occurs when we break a spiritual law—it is the inevitable reaping of what we have sown.

The sickly spiritual condition of so many Christians is not, as they sometimes think, a direct infliction of God's displeasure. It is simply and only the necessary consequence of the unsuitable and indigestible spiritual food upon which they have been feeding.

EVERYDAY RELIGION: Ch. 2

My Father, is it possible you have been preparing a spiritual feast for me, and all I see is desert and rocks and dryness? Is the irritation or boredom I feel really a wilderness of my own making?

Walk with me now, Father, by your Spirit, through the dead, dry places in me. Show me how I can be fed and strengthened, today, by your hand.

12
Jesus, Bread of Life

Jesus [said], "The work of God is this: to believe in
the one he has sent." . . . So [the disciples] asked him,
"What miraculous sign then will you give that we
may see it and believe you?" . . .
Then Jesus declared, "I am the bread of life. He who
comes to me will never go hungry . . . whoever comes
to me I will never drive away."

John 6:29–30, 35, 37

What is the proper food for the soul? What is
the "daily bread" the Lord would have us eat?

Jesus tells us, in that wonderful discourse in
John 6, when He says plainly, "I am the bread of
life. Whoever eats my flesh and drinks my blood
has eternal life" (v.53).

To many Christians, this is a mysterious
passage, and I do not feel at all competent to
explain it theologically. But it has a commonsense
side as well, a practical application for our
everyday lives.

Very few people realize the effect of their own

thoughts upon the condition of their soul. Our thoughts are, in fact, our soul's food. They are the substance from which evolve our inner strength and health and beauty—or which cause us to become weak, unhealthy and deformed. The things we think about are the things we feed upon. If we think low and corrupt thoughts, we bring diseases upon our soul just as surely as we bring diseases upon our body by eating corrupted foods or foods lacking in nutrition.

The man or woman who thinks constantly of "self," feeds on self. . . . This one will at last become puffed up with self and suffer from the dreadful disease of conceit, or self-importance.

On the other hand, if we think of Christ, our soul "feeds" on Christ. We eat His flesh and drink His blood in the practical sense by filling our souls with believing thoughts of Him. . . . I know that anyone who tries this will quickly find that they do feed upon Him, to the joy and delight of their hearts!

If we take the words of God, His revealed truth, into our lips and eat them—that is, if we dwell on His words, speak them to ourselves over and over, thoroughly take them in and assimilate their meaning in a practical way—then we will find our souls nourished, made strong, full of vigor. . . . If we think on pure and lovely things, we will grow pure and lovely like them.

This cannot mean that we are to be consciously thinking of Christ every minute. This is not possible, nor is it desirable. But it does mean that we are to have taken in and digested the thoughts of Christ instead of our own, so that we come to look at things as He does. That we measure, weigh, and judge as He judges.

We can do, with Jesus, as we would do if we were the disciples of any great master in art or science whose spirit we want to assimilate and whose works we want to reproduce. We can study His life, and understand the Spirit in which He came, and thoroughly fill our souls with His ideas. In short, we make Him our constant companion in mind and in spirit. We live with Him and in Him. And so He lives in us.

Here is the "work" we must do, our spiritual "feast": To think on Jesus so that underlying thoughts of your heart—the thoughts that lie at the bottom of all other thoughts, the thoughts that motivate all you do and say—be of the Lord himself, and of all His infinite goodness and love.

No, it is not possible to literally have Him consciously in your thoughts every moment. But rather, fix the very life of your soul in Him, down at the bottom of all your thoughts, and this will become a solid foundation upon which your whole life will rest.

Accept all His ideas, and make them your own.

EVERYDAY RELIGION: Ch. 2

My Father, you who are my one Provider. . . .

I come to you now, to feed my soul on the love-feast that you give me.

I fix my eyes on Jesus, born of flesh, with miracles in His hands. I look upon His cross . . . His blood . . . and the light breaking from His empty tomb!

In this quiet moment, I bow in the presence of my Risen Lord. . . .

13
The Lord Most High

I . . . will sing praise to the name of the Lord Most High.

Psalm 7:17

I am poor [in spirit] . . . thy salvation, O God, [will] set me up on high.

Psalm 69:29, KJV

*M*y beloved friend . . . I am writing to give you a plain, unvarnished statement of the facts. You can make out of them what you please.

Recently, we were obliged to hold a "Convention for the Promotion of Holiness." And to be honest, we never felt for a moment as if we were serving the Lord in this . . . though we concluded He would not be angry with us if we agreed, because our friends pressed us so much.

As for me, I have come to the place where I

only want the will of God to be done under all circumstances, and I really don't care what His will is. I felt utterly indifferent to the convention in every way—except that it was a great trial to leave the comforts of my home and have to travel so far.

We had made no preparations for the meeting; we neither studied, nor prayed, nor meditated. . . . True, when the time came for us to speak we meant to do our best. . . . I cannot imagine a meeting begun in a worse frame of mind.

There was no enthusiasm on my part. Our own words were, to me, a bore. . . . I was sure that any honest chronicler of the event would say, "No wonder the meetings were an utter failure."

But I must keep to the baffling facts: The convention was a perfect success.

God's power and His blessings came, despite our feelings. There was every sign of the continual presence of the Spirit. Men and women rushed to give their lives to the Lord. Many who had abandoned the faith returned eagerly, fervently to Him. Christians who had been cold and halfhearted were fairly tripping over each other to commit everything to God. Everyone present was experiencing some great blessing, in wave after wave . . . and after, I was overwhelmed with people who wanted to know how to go deeper in the spiritual life.

Who would dream of such an outcome to the

indifference we felt beforehand and could not shake from ourselves?

All I can make of it is this: I feel myself to have got out into a limitless ocean of the love of God that overflows all things. My faith is complete if you but grant me an all-powerful and just Creator. I need nothing more.

No religious fervency or "tricks."

UNPUBLISHED LETTER: August 8, 1876

My Father, show me if a subtle pride has crept into my faith . . . if I have placed my trust in my spiritual understanding, my religious performance . . . my self. . . .

Remind me that when I "raise up myself" I fall— and every honor and every blessing that comes my way is a gift from you.

14
"Jesus Saves Me Now"

*J*esus said, ". . . take heart! I have overcome the
world."

———

John 16:33

*. . . pay attention to [the words of our Lord], as to a
light shining in a dark place, until the day dawns and
the morning star rises in your hearts.*

———

2 Peter 1:19

*T*here came a time when I had to commit the
whole matter of my dark, rebellious human spirit
to the Lord—that spirit within me that wanted to
tell the Lord how to do things my way, that was
rubbed raw at the very thought of giving a godly
response when my "rights" and "desires" were
bruised by anyone.

I told the Lord I could not conquer this
attitude in myself, and that He must conquer it

for me, if ever it was to be accomplished. And then I stood aside, as it were, and let the battle begin.

And battle it was. . . .

There soon came a day when a guest had come to stay with us, a most imposing person whose impositions were many and entirely unjustifiable. I was angry and was tempted to go into a fit of sulks. And just to show my displeasure I thought I might be sulky for a week or two.

But the moment the temptation came, I knew the way of escape. And I rushed off to be alone somewhere that I might fight the battle out. (Though I admit I was so boiling over with feeling provoked that I could not walk quietly, but ran up to my bedroom, slamming the doors after me.)

When safe in the seclusion of my room, I knelt down and said, "Lord, I am provoked. I want to be provoked. I know I ought not to be provoked, though, and I want to rule over my own spirit. I hand this whole matter over to you, because I cannot fight this battle. You must fight it for me."

And then I declared, over and over, "Jesus saves me now!"

You must know that I said these words out of a heart that seemed brimful of rebellion. By all appearances I was declaring a lie when I said the Lord saved me, for I was not behaving saved, and it did not look likely I could be. But by faith I laid hold of it, and declared even in the midst of turmoil that the Lord could and did save me now.

And presently, as I continued in this manner of prayer, a summer morning of peace and contentment slowly spread within me. All my resentment began to evaporate as the morning dew. I felt as happy as a bird in the light of a new-rising sun, even for the very thing that had caused my provocation.

In this way, God proves that He is able to deliver our souls when we trust Him.

Jesus said that He has overcome the world; not we. And He will always overcome, when we will put a matter into His hands.

THE UNSELFISHNESS OF GOD: Ch. 26

My Father, you know the many dark pockets full of selfish rights I have kept for my own.

Today, when I am bruised in any way, call me to yourself . . . destroy the darkness in me . . . and rise in me as the morning star . . . in peace.

15

The Fact of Our Freedom

The reason the Son of God appeared was to destroy the devil's work.

1 John 3:8

Jesus returned to Galilee in the power of the Spirit. . . . The scroll of the prophet Isaiah was handed to him. Unrolling it, he [read]: "The Spirit of the Lord is on me . . . to release the oppressed, to proclaim the year of the Lord's favor."

Luke 4:14, 17–19

A keen observer once said to me, "You Christians seem to have religion that makes you miserable. You are like a man with a headache. He does not want to get rid of his head, but it hurts him to keep it. How can you expect outsiders to want something that causes you yourselves so much discomfort?"

75

I saw, as in a flash, that the religion of Christ ought to be—and was meant to be—something that does not make men miserable, but a life that makes them happy.

How unhappy is the real, spiritual experience of so many Christians. Their victories are few and fleeting, their defeats many and disastrous. They do not live as they believe children of God ought to live. They may have a clear understanding of doctrinal truths, but have not come into any possession of the life and power within these doctrines. They speak joyfully in their head knowledge of the things revealed in Scripture— but they have not experienced in reality the very truths Scripture reveals.

These people believe in Christ, they talk about Him and serve Him—but they cannot seem to find Him as their soul's true and nourishing life. They have not found Him within, abiding there forever, revealing himself continually in His beauty.

So it is that you may have found Jesus as your Savior from the penalty of sin, but you have not found Him as Savior from its power . . . your soul is starving and dying within you, and you cry out in secret again and again for that bread and water of life which you see promised in the Scriptures to all believers.

Is this all the Lord had in mind when He laid down His precious life to deliver you? . . . Did He intend to leave you struggling under a weary

consciousness of defeat and discouragement? . . .
When all those declarations were made
concerning His coming and the work He was to
accomplish, did they mean only this that you
have so far experienced?

The Bible tells us that the Son of God came to
destroy the works of the evil one. Can we allow
ourselves to believe that this is beyond His
power—that He came, but to His great dismay,
found that He was unable to accomplish His
plan?

Settle down on this fact:

Jesus came to save you, now, in this life, from
the power and dominion of sin—to make you
more than conquerors through His power.

THE CHRISTIAN'S SECRET OF A HAPPY LIFE: Ch. 1

*My Father, today, I will not feed on
my doubts . . . for that will imprison my spirit.*

*I will seize upon on the fact that your kingdom of
righteousness has come . . . that I may live strong and
run free.*

16
Living in the Present Moment

For as high as the heavens are above the earth, so great is [God's] love . . . as far as the east is from the west, so far has he removed our transgressions from us.

———

Psalm 103:11–12

Now the Lord is the Spirit, and where the Spirit of the Lord is, there is freedom. And we, who with unveiled faces all reflect the Lord's glory, are being transformed into his likeness with ever-increasing glory. . . .

———

2 Corinthians 3:17–18

Discouragement at any personal failure is always a greater fault than the failure itself.

It is all right to see the failure, if there has been one, but the moment it is seen it must be confessed and left with the Lord and forgotten (1 John 1:9).

Discouragement at our own failures is one of Satan's greatest weapons against us, and the only way to baffle him is to do what I say—and so I repeat: confess, be forgiven, and forget the whole thing.

It is the rule of my life never to think over and over and over again about any past action. This saves me all temptations to self-elation—that is, the mistake of thinking that I and my sins are so greatly important that God is preoccupying himself over them. It saves me all temptations to discouragement.

And thus, I am able to live continually in the present moment with God.

Fenelon says, "Make it a rule, at the close of every action, to end all reflection upon it, whether of joy or sadness. . . . When we are no longer embarrassed by these restless reflections upon self, we begin to enjoy true liberty.

"The chagrin we feel at our own defects is in fact . . . the outcome of a despairing self-love. . . . Nothing marks so decidedly the solid progress of a soul, as that it is enabled to view its own depravity without being disturbed or discouraged.

"You will find by experience how much your spiritual progress will be aided by a simple, peaceful turning to God."

Unpublished letter: January 22, 1882

My Creator-Father, you call me a new creation . . . and I am!

You know my wounds and my sins . . . and you know that I am but dust. Today, I come to you without hesitation or shame . . . in need of healing . . . deep . . . sweet . . . and cleansing.

17
Holy Spirit, Our Power

We have not received the spirit of the world but the Spirit who is from God, that we may understand what God has freely given us.

1 Corinthians 2:12

Jews look for miraculous signs and Greeks look for wisdom, but we preach Christ crucified . . . to those whom God has called . . . Christ [is] the power of God and the wisdom of God.

1 Corinthians 1:23–24

. . . be filled with the Spirit. . . .

Ephesians 5:18

The baptism of the Holy Spirit is to me the crowning point in all Christian experience. Right views concerning it are of great importance.

Unfortunately, it seems to be a subject beset with difficulties and errors, though evidently it was intended to be one of the simplest and most easily understood of all. . . .

What does it mean to be baptized with the Holy Spirit?

The word *baptize* means to immerse, to dip into. . . . to be baptized with the Holy Spirit means to be immersed into the Spirit of God. It is described in various ways:

Partakers of the divine nature (2 Peter 1:4): having Christ swell in the heart by faith (Ephesians 3:17); . . . being a dwelling place for God through the Spirit (Ephesians 2:22).

To be filled with the Holy Spirit means simply to open every aspect of our lives to him, holding back nothing at all, until we are filled with God. . . .

It is plain that the expression "baptism of the Holy Spirit" has no exclusive meaning—that no Christian whosoever is excluded—but is only one way of describing the fact of our abiding in Christ and His abiding in us: This *is* the life hidden with Christ in God. . . .

Herein lies the mistake that is too often made these days: the "baptism of the Spirit" is looked upon as an *experience* rather than a life; we are taught that it is a gift God will bestow if we seek it in certain ways. Rather, I would tell you, it is an accomplished fact, and we may root our spirits in it, expecting to draw more and more inward life from the Holy Spirit.

The Scripture plainly teaches that the gift of the Holy Spirit is a universal gift to all believers, and without it we cannot be believers at all . . . (see John 3:5–6). . . . In Galatians we read, "Because you are sons, God sent the Spirit of His Son into our hearts, the Spirit who calls out *Abba*. Father!" (4:6). . . .

We must believe, therefore, that this unspeakable gift, which is meant to help us enter into the glorious realms of the Spirit *now*, is already the possession of even the weakest and most failing child of God. It is true, whether we recognize His presence or not, whether we acknowledge and obey His control or not. He *is* within each of us. . . .

The secret is that we must allow Him to take full possession. We *are* His sanctuary, His dwelling place, although we may not yet have opened every inward chamber of our hearts to let Him dwell therein.

And so, in seeking the "baptism of the Holy Spirit", understand that it is not a new thing you ask for. But simply recognize the presence of God already within you, and fully submit to His ownership, and allow Him to control every circumstance.

The Holy Spirit is, I say, a gift—but to be immersed in the Holy Spirit is not a gift. It is a command. . . . Sunlight is a gift, but letting the sunlight into our homes is a privilege and a joy. To be baptized with the sunlight is merely to get into it, and not to shut ourselves away in glooms of doubt, self-will, discouragement.

To be baptized with the Holy Spirit is just the same.

THE CHRISTIAN'S SECRET OF A HAPPY LIFE: Ch. 15

My Father, you who are the Spirit and Life itself . . .

Show me "rooms" of my life where I am still in possession . . . in control. . . .

Today, despite any spiritual gifts I mistakenly think I possess, I acknowledge my silly powerlessness . . . and open myself to your true right and ownership over all of me.

18
Strongholds of Doubt

The weapons we fight with are not the weapons of the world. On the contrary, they have divine power to demolish strongholds. We demolish arguments and every pretention that sets itself up against the knowledge of God, and we take captive every thought to make it obedient to Christ.

2 Corinthians 10:4–5

. . . he who doubts is like a wave of the sea . . . he is a double-minded man, unstable in all he does.

James 1:6, 8

Jesus replied, ". . . have faith and do not doubt. . . ."

Matthew 21:21

To have doubts arise is not sinful.
But from the beginning to the end of your

Christian life it is always sinful to indulge doubts—that is, to mull them over and over in your mind until they paralyze you in spirit, and kill the life of God in you. Doubts and discouragements are all from an evil source and are always untrue.

A direct and emphatic denial is the only way to meet a doubt.

Deliverance from the fatal habit of doubt occurs by the same means as deliverance from any other sin. . . . You must hand over your doubting to Christ as you would any other temptation. You must do with it what you must do with your temper and pride—that is, give it up to the Lord.

I myself believe the only effectual remedy for every sin, including doubt, is to take a pledge against it, just as a person who is overcome by alcohol must take the pledge against drinking, trusting wholly in the Lord alone to keep you steadfast.

Like any other sin, the stronghold is in the will, and the will to doubt must be surrendered. . . . God always takes possession of a surrendered will. If we make up our minds and say that we will not doubt, and if we surrender this central fortress within our human nature, that very moment His Spirit will begin to work in us all the good pleasure of His will.

The trouble in this matter of doubting is that the Christian does not always make a full

surrender. He is apt to reserve a little secret
liberty to doubt, looking upon it as being
sometimes a necessity.

The liberty to doubt must be given up forever.
We must consent to a continuous life of inevitable
trust.

Let doubts clamor outside the fortress of your
will, once it is given over to God. They cannot
hurt you if you will not let them in.

Sometimes it will seem as though you were
shutting your door against your best friend, and
your heart will long for your doubts. . . . But
deny yourself. Take up your cross in this matter,
and quietly but firmly refuse to listen to a single
word.

THE CHRISTIAN'S SECRET OF A HAPPY LIFE: Ch. 9

*My Father, give me ears to hear and
eyes to see the way of the Spirit as it opens before me.*

*Is it because I want to "protect" myself from hurt
and disappointment—is that why I hold back from
trusting completely in you?*

19
The Prison of Discouragement

. . . the Lord . . . the God of your fathers told you. . . . "Do not be afraid. Do not be discouraged."

Deuteronomy 1:21

I know that nothing good lives in me, that is, in my sinful nature. For I have the desire to do what is good, but I cannot carry it out. . . . Who will rescue me. . . ? Thanks be to God—through Jesus Christ our Lord!

Romans 7:18, 24–25

Scripture weaves together for us many sound, strong declarations from the Lord:

"I am your Creator and Redeemer. I am your strength and wisdom. I am your ever-present and all-knowing God. And I will be with you to protect you through everything. No enemy will hurt you; no evil thing spoken about you will

91

disturb you. My presence will be your safety and your sure defense."

You would think that, in the face of such assertions, not even the most fainthearted among us could find a single loophole to allow for discouragement. But discouragement comes in many subtle forms. Our spiritual enemies attack us in many disguises.

Our own special makeup and temperament is one of the most common and insidious of our enemies. We tell ourselves, "Other people are just made differently—it's possible for them to be cheerful and courageous. But it's all right for me to be discouraged considering the way I'm made—so foolish, helpless and weak. How could God expect me to be able to overcome?"

There would be ample cause for discouragement—if we were called upon to fight our battles ourselves. We would be right in thinking we could not do it. But if the Lord is to fight the battles for us . . . this puts an entirely different face on the matter!

If this is the case—and indeed it is—then our inability to fight becomes an advantage instead of a disadvantage. For we can only be strong in the Lord when we are weak in ourselves.

In reality, in the life of the spirit, our human weakness is our greatest strength.

GOD OF ALL COMFORT: Ch. 13

My Mighty Father, *there you are—in your heavenly fortress of strength and joy!*

And here I am—often stumbling through battlefields that seem littered with my failures.

Show me if I have allowed myself "loopholes" . . . if there are deeper motives, secret reasons, why I have let myself fail.

20
The "High Places" In God

Out of the depths I cry to you. . . . O Lord, hear
my voice.

Psalm 130:1–2

As the Father has loved me, so have I loved you.
Now remain in my love.

John 15:9

Until the day breaks, and the shadows flee, I will go
to the mountain. . . .

Song of Songs 4:6

*T*he loneliness thou speaks of I know all about. For do not think . . . that it is confined to unmarried people. It is just as real in lives that have plenty of human ties, husbands and children, and friends.

95

It is the loneliness of this world's life, the loneliness of hearts that are made for union with God, but which have not yet fully realized it. . . . I believe God has ordained it in the very nature of things by creating us for himself alone. And I believe He very rarely allows any human love to be satisfying, just so that this loneliness may drive us to Him.

I have noticed that where human love is satisfying, something always comes in to spoil it. Either there is death, or there is separation, or there is a change of feeling on one side or the other . . . and the heart is driven out of its human resting place on to God alone.

Sometimes God permits a little taste of a satisfying love to a human being, but I do not believe it ever lasts long. I do not mean that the love may not last, but separation comes in some way, and the perfect satisfaction is taken out of it.

If thou can only see this and settle down to it, it will help thee very much to rise in your faith. Thou wilt give up, as I have, any expectation of finding satisfaction in the creature, and will no longer suffer with disappointment at not finding it.

I am speaking . . . out of the depths of my own experience when I say this, and thee may believe me.

UNPUBLISHED LETTER: January 8, 1882

My Father, I know there are deep and lonely places in me that no human love can fill. Strongholds of doubt. Prisons of discouragement.

Now, in this quiet moment, I listen for your voice . . . for assurances that you care for me.

I ask to know your high and holy Presence which is total rest . . . and freedom.

21
All Are His Servants

Your word, O Lord, is eternal; it stands firm in the heavens. Your faithfulness continues through all generations; you established the earth and it endures. Your laws endure to this day, for all things serve you.

Psalm 119:89–91

Once you were alienated from God and were enemies in your minds because of your evil behavior. But now he has reconciled you . . . to present you holy in his sight . . . if you continue in your faith, established and firm, not moved from the hope held out in the gospel.

Colossians 1:21–23

*A*ll things are His servants. Not a few things only, but all things. Not things on Sunday only, but things on weekdays as well.

We generally think that only the good people

or the good things of life can serve God but here the psalmist tells us that all things whether good or bad are His servants. That is to say, all things—no matter what their origin may be—are used by the Lord to accomplish His purposes, and all are made to work together for good to them who are called according to His purposes (Romans 8:28).

Both the psalmist and the apostle spoke out of some of the darkest problems and mysteries of life when they made these declarations. . . . But for both men, it was their profound faith in the God who created and controls the world that enabled them to see through the blinding mysteries. They knew for certain this magnificent fact: All things are His servants and must therefore work to the good of His children.

"Praise the Lord from the earth, you great sea creatures and all ocean depths, lightning and hail, snow and clouds, stormy winds that do his bidding . . ." (Psalm 148:7–8). Even lightning and hail, snow and storm clouds, creatures of the sea and the terrifying power of the oceans— everything fulfills God's word and serves Him.

Not only is this true of the fierce and cruel things of nature, but of the wicked things in man as well. "Surely the wrath of man shall praise thee: the remainder of wrath shalt thou restrain" (Psalm 76:10, KJV). The "wrath of man" is altogether a wrong thing—but even this becomes

God's servant and is forced to accomplish His purposes.

The death of our Lord Jesus Christ on the cross is a luminous illustration of this truth. It was certainly by "wicked hands" that He was nailed to a cross and put to death. And yet these hands accomplished—unbeknown to themselves—God's predetermined plan for our salvation!

And so I believe it is always. All things are used by God as His servants, let the agencies that started them be what they may. God in no way inaugurates evil, but when evil from any source is directed against His children, He makes it His "servant" to carry them a blessing.

We will know this to be true the very instant we understand from the depths of our soul, what is the nature of God's relationship to us.

His care for us is more watchful and more tender than the care of any human father could possibly be.

Repeat the words over and over again. This God—whom all things must serve whether they know Him or not—He is our Father!

EVERYDAY RELIGION: Ch. 5

My Father, Lord of All,
. . . *am I still, in some ways, behaving like an "enemy of God"?*

101

Show me where I am fighting against you—where my desires are colliding against some circumstance or person, who is sent in your service. I stand firm in the certainty that in you, my Father, no evil can come to me.

22
God of All Comfort

Praise be to the God and Father of our Lord Jesus Christ, the Father of compassion and the God of all comfort, who comforts us in all our troubles. . . .

2 Corinthians 1:3–4

Comfort, comfort my people," says your God.

Isaiah 40:1

Among all the names that reveal God, this one—the "God of all comfort"—seems to me the loveliest and the most absolutely comforting.

However full of discomforts the outward life of the followers of such a God might be, their inward spiritual life must surely be one of comfort, always and under all circumstances. But in fact, it often seems as if exactly the opposite were the case. It seems that the spiritual lives of

103

many, many of God's children are full of the utmost discomfort.

This discomfort arises from anxiety—a deep unsettledness—as to their relationship to God, and from their doubts about His love for them.

Many people torment themselves with the thought that they are too good-for-nothing to be worthy of His care. And many secretly suspect Him of being indifferent to their hurt and suffering, or they believe He has abandoned them just at the moment of crisis, when they need Him most.

Then there are those who feel anxious and unsettled about everything pertaining to their spiritual life—about their moods and feelings, their indifference to the Bible, their lack of enthusiasm for prayer, their coldness of heart. They are tormented with regrets over their past, and devoured with anxieties about the future. Because of all these things, they feel unworthy to enter God's presence, and cannot believe they really belong to Him.

Christians like this can be happy and comfortable with their human friends, but they cannot be happy or comfortable with God.

"God of all comfort"? . . . We have failed to believe it. It seems to us too good to be true . . . more than our suspicious natures can take in. We may hope sometimes for little scraps of comfort. Why do we run frightened away from the "all comfort" that is ours in the salvation of the Lord Jesus Christ?

"As a mother comforts her child, so will I comfort you; and you will be comforted . . ." (Isaiah 66:13).

It is real comforting that is meant here, the sort that a child feels when it is held on its mother's knee or on her hip. And yet how many of us really believe that God's comforting is actually as tender and true as a mother's, or even half or quarter so real?

We have, rather, been inclined to look upon Him as a stern, unbending Judge—one who holds us at a distance, who demands our respectful homage, who is critical of our slightest fault. Is it any wonder then that in our spiritual lives we are so thoroughly uncomfortable?

I rejoice to tell you: The stern Judge is not there, He does not exist!

The God who does exist is the God and Father of our Lord Jesus Christ, the God who so loved the world that He sent His Son, not to judge the world but to save it (John 3:16–17). He is the God who "anointed" the Lord Jesus Christ to bind up the brokenhearted, and to proclaim liberty to captives, and to comfort all that mourn (Luke 4:18). . . . Not a few select ones only, but all. . . .

Throughout His life on earth, Jesus fulfilled this divine mission. When His disciples asked Him to call down fire from heaven to consume some people who refused to receive Him, Jesus turned and rebuked them: "You do not know what kind of spirit you are of, for the Son of Man did not come to destroy lives but to save them" (Luke 9:55).

I love to meditate on such a mission of comfort in a world of mourning such as ours. And I long to see every downcast and sorrowful heart comforted with this comforting of God.

THE GOD OF ALL COMFORT: Ch. 3

God of All Comfort, My Father!

Open my spiritual understanding today . . . so that I will know once and for all that the troubles which come at me are not proofs of your "judgment" . . . not evidences that you have abandoned me.

Touch that one place in me, now, that most needs your comfort. . . .

23
Shaking

Once more I will shake not only the earth but also the heavens," [declares the Lord]. The words "once more" indicate the removing of what can be shaken— that is, created things—so that what cannot be shaken may remain. Therefore, since we are receiving a kingdom that cannot be shaken, let us be thankful . . . for our "God is a consuming fire."

—————

Hebrews 12:26–29

Endure hardship as discipline; God is treating you as sons. . . . No discipline seems pleasant at the time, but painful. Later on, however, it produces a harvest of righteousness and peace. . . .

—————

Hebrews 12:7, 11

If love sees those it loves going wrong, it must, because it is love, do what it can to save them. Any supposed love that would fail to do this is really only selfishness.

Because of His unfathomable love, the God of

love, when He sees His children resting their souls on things that can be shaken, must necessarily remove those things from their lives. It is one of His ways to drive us to rest only on eternal things that cannot be shaken. Admittedly, this process of removing is sometimes very hard.

It is very possible, even for the Christian, to build a spiritual home—that true place where our soul goes to find rest and peace—on insecure and unsafe foundations. When storms beat upon such a house, the ruin of it is great (see Matthew 7:24–27).

For many, their spiritual experience seems firm and steady enough when all is going well in life. But they find themselves tottering and falling when difficulties come.

Of course, the immediate thought that leaps to mind for most Christians is that our spiritual lives must be "built upon the rock of Jesus Christ." True enough. But have we any idea what we mean when we so glibly use that expression? It seems to me this is one of those religious phrases that is used so often, without any clue as to its meaning.

I suspect that if we were perfectly honest with ourselves we would often find that our dependence is almost wholly upon other things— on having right moods and feelings, on believing right doctrines or dogmas, on whatever else constitutes security to us. Yes, if we were honest, most of us would find that the idea of Christ himself, as the only rock on which we depend, is of altogether secondary importance.

The apostle tells us that the things that are shaken are the "things that are made"—that is, the things that are manufactured by our own efforts, feelings that we stir up, doctrines that we elaborate, good works that we perform.

It is not that these things are bad in themselves. It is only when the soul begins to rest on them instead of upon the Lord that He is compelled to "shake" us from off them.

So there may be times in our spiritual lives when we feel as settled and immovable as the roots of a mountain. But there comes an upheaval, and all our foundations are shaken and thrown down. We are ready to despair, and question whether or not we can be Christian at all.

It was at just such a moment that my own soul caught its first real sight of God. What seemed certain spiritual ruin and defeat was turned into triumph.

THE GOD OF ALL COMFORT: Ch. 11

My True Father, I do feel the shaking. But I will stand firm in my trust in you today . . . and I feel your bracing arm around my shoulders.

24
The Giant "I"

I thought to myself, "Look, I have grown and increased in wisdom more than anyone. . . ." I applied myself to the understanding of wisdom . . . but I learned that this, too, is a chasing after the wind.

———

Ecclesiastes 1:16–17

If anyone thinks he is something when he is nothing, he deceives himself. Each one should test his own actions. Then he can take pride in himself. . . .

———

Galatians 6:3–5

To almost everyone, the greatest person in the world is himself. Our whole lives are made up of endless variations of the word *me*: What do people think of *me*? How will this situation affect *me*? Will this make *me* happy? Do people respect *me* as they should? Look at *my* wealth. Behold *my* remarkable experiences. Listen to *my* wisdom. Adopt *my* views. Follow *my* methods. And so on, through the whole range of life.

Always and everywhere, the giant *I* intrudes itself, demanding attention and insisting on its rights.

Like Solomon writing in Ecclesiastes, we remark to ourselves all the time about our various greatnesses—our wisdom, our learning, our righteousness, our good works. We are profoundly impressed with their value and importance, and we want everyone around us to notice.

The whole book of Ecclesiastes is founded on this devotion to the word "I". . . . Solomon tried to solve the problem of earthly happiness, seeking for the true purpose of living. He obtained everything he thought would make him happy and secure. But in the end, he declared that all his accomplishments brought him only to deeper and deeper emptiness.

This must be the inevitable result of everything that has *I* and *I* only for its center. . . . Have you discovered this yet in your own spiritual experience?

I is a most exacting person, requiring the best seats and the highest places for itself—feeling terribly wounded and offended if its claims are not recognized and its rights considered:

My rights have been stepped on.
No one considered *me*, or *my* opinion.

How much there is of this sort of thing (said

outright, or secretly thought) in the heart where the *I* is king!

Lowliness of mind is the only true road to spiritual honor. Only he who humbles himself will be exalted (1 Peter 5:6). Our own divine Master has set this example for us, and if we really want to have the mind of Christ Jesus we must be willing to be made of no reputation and must take, not the place of mastery, but the place of service (see Philippians 2:3–8).

Now to become lowly in heart I must get rid of the *I* in my life. This has nothing to do, as some people think, with saying bitter and disparaging things about myself. I am convinced that the giant *I* is quite as much exalted and puffed-up by self-blame as by self-praise. . . . Self is so greedy of notice that, if it cannot be praised, it would rather be blamed than not noticed at all! . . . If it feels a delicacy about saying, "I am so good," it finds almost as much delight in saying, "I am so bad."

The Apostle Paul understood the common sense of true humility. . . . He bids goodbye to his own gigantic *I* when he cries out, "I am crucified with Christ: nevertheless I live; yet not I, but Christ liveth in me" (Galatians 2:20, KJV).

This declaration—"yet not I"—is one of those swords of the Spirit about which Paul speaks when he describes the Christian's armor (Ephesians 6:10–17). I know of none that is more effective in our conflict with the unruly giant *I*.

Not even a giant can resist the disintegrating process that will occur when we absolutely, persistently, ignore its existence.

EVERYDAY RELIGION: Ch. 6

My Father, how hard it is to look past this giant "I" which rises again and again, like a pillar, blocking my path to you.

"I" come to you now . . . surrendering my self-interests.

And though it feels like a fearsome crucifixion, I know that beyond this surrender to your will . . . is a new-risen life in you.

25
Risky Paths

As the heavens are higher than the earth, so are my ways higher than your ways and my thoughts than your thoughts . . . my word that goes out from my mouth . . . will not return to me empty. . . ."

Isaiah 55:9, 11

Suppose you give yourself to the Lord—to be wholly and altogether His, made and molded according to His own divine purpose, determined to follow Him wherever He may lead you. It is just at this point that you are faced with a new and very practical difficulty.

How are you to know the voice of the Good Shepherd, whom you have pledged to follow?

Many Christians live in constant doubt and confusion as to His will for them.

And this confusion is further compounded. Maybe there are certain "paths" into which God seems to be calling you, of which your friends disapprove—and it may be that these disapproving friends are older than yourself in the Christian life. You can hardly bear to disagree with them, or to see the distress on their faces.

The first thing you must do is to ask the Lord to help you quietly examine the motives of your heart. Be sure that you really have set your will to obey the Lord in every respect. If this is your purpose then, and your soul is merely waiting to know the will of God in order to consent to it, then you have done your part.

From this point, you can be certain that He will make His mind known to you and will guide you on the right paths, for "He calls his own sheep by name and leads them out . . . he goes on ahead of them, and his sheep follow him because they know his voice" (John 10:3–4). . . . And, "If any of you lacks wisdom, he should ask God, who gives generously to all without finding fault, and it will be given to him" (James 1:5).

Let no hint of doubt turn you from a steadfast faith in God's willingness and ability to guide you.

Remember this though: Our God has all knowledge and all wisdom. Therefore it is very possible He may guide you into paths wherein He knows great blessings are awaiting you just around the next fearsome turn—paths on which, to our short-sighted human eyes, there seems to be only confusion and loss.

You must become settled on this spiritual fact: God's thoughts are not like man's thoughts, nor are His ways like our ways. He alone, who knows the end of things from their beginning, is able to determine what the results of any course of action may be.

THE CHRISTIAN'S SECRET OF A HAPPY LIFE: Ch. 8

My Steadfast Father, I know you've been calling me to risk something—in a relationship, in my work, with my family—and I have been stuck "calculating" the outcome.

Today, I ask you to be my guarding Shepherd, so I can give up the wearying task of protecting myself from possible hurt. Let me hear you clearly . . . trust the end to you from the beginning . . . and then follow. . . .

26
Darkness That Shines

. . . hide me in the shadow of your wings from the
wicked who assail me. . . .

Psalm 17:8–9

He will cover you with his feathers, and under his
wings you will find refuge. . . . If you make the Most
High your dwelling—even the Lord, who is my
refuge—then no harm will befall you. . . .

Psalm 91:4, 9–10

If I say, "Surely the darkness will hide me and the
light become night around me," even the darkness will
not be dark to you; the night will shine like the day,
for darkness is as light to you.

Psalm 139:11–12

I could not speak of the scandalous charges

119

circulating in Europe and America about my husband, not while there was any hope. . . . Now however that hope is vain, and I may therefore speak openly of our trials, and of my dear husband's bitter suffering.

My dear husband has been most cruelly treated, and the Lord's cause has suffered a sad blow through the mistakes of some whom my husband supposed to be his warmest friends. I do not however blame them. They have meant to do right, and they could have had no power at all against him, unless God had permitted it, so I am able to look entirely away from "second causes" and to receive all that has come to us from the hands of God, and to say continually "Thy will be done."

Our friends in this country all know my dear husband too well to believe for one moment the wicked slanders that come from England concerning him, and they have all drawn closer to him than ever. This is a great comfort to him, but he is a heartbroken man and will never, I fear, recover anything of his old energy or health.

As for myself, the effect of this has been to teach me to rest more utterly and more blindly than ever in the sweet will of God. No one ever committed themselves and their lives more completely to the Lord than we did; and since He has permitted this, it must be for the best, dark as it looks.

I feel just like a little chick that has run out of

a storm and under its mothers wings, and is safe there. I hear the raging of the storm, and I am utterly unable to comprehend it or to measure the damage it is doing. But I am safe "under His wings," and there I must rest.

He can manage the dark storm, I cannot. Why then should I worry or be anxious?

UNPUBLISHED LETTER: February 24, 1876

My Father of Light, what situation have I been calling "dark" . . . that you want me to enter into unreservedly . . . uncomplaining . . . so that you may show your great brightness?

27
The Chariots of God

Who may ascend the hill of the Lord? Who may stand in his holy place? He . . . who does not lift up his soul . . . to what is false.

Psalm 24:3–4

The Lord said to Job: "Would you discredit my justice? Would you condemn me to justify yourself?"

Job 40:1, 8

*E*arthly cares are a heavenly discipline.

But they are something even better than a discipline. They are God's chariots, sent to take the soul to its high places of triumph.

They do not look like chariots. They look instead like enemies, sufferings, trials, defeats, misunderstandings, disappointments, unkindnesses. They look like "vehicles" that are dangerously out of control, crashing toward us with misery and wretchedness, about to roll over us and crush us. But if we could see them as they really are, we should recognize them as chariots of triumph in which we may ride to the very high heights of victory for which our souls have been longing and praying.

The dangerous "vehicle" is the visible thing; the chariot of God is the invisible.

The King of Syria came up against the man of God with horses and chariots that could be seen plainly by anyone—but God had chariots that could be seen by none, except those looking with the eyes of faith. The prophet's servant could only see the outward and visible, and he cried in dismay—as so many have done since—"Oh master, what shall we do?" But the prophet sat calmly within his house, without fear, because his eyes were opened to see the invisible. All he asked for his servant was, "Lord, open his eyes so he may see" (2 Kings 6:8–19).

This is the prayer we need to pray for ourselves, and for one another: "Lord, open our eyes that we may see!" For the world all around us is teeming with God's horses and chariots waiting to carry us to places of glorious victory. And when our eyes are opened to the spiritual world, we shall see all the events of life—whether small or great, whether joyful or sad—as chariots for our souls.

Here is the secret: Everything that comes to us becomes a chariot the moment we treat it as such. . . . That misunderstanding, that thing that feels like death itself, that unkindness, that disappointment, that loss, that defeat—all are chariots, waiting to carry you to the very heights of victory you have so longed to reach. . . . On the other hand, even the smallest trial becomes one of those out-of-control vehicles to crush you in misery and despair. If you let it.

The high heavenly places toward which we are headed are interior, not exterior. And the road that leads to them is interior also. . . . It lies within each one of us to choose which it shall be.

THE CHRISTIAN'S SECRET OF A HAPPY LIFE: Ch. 18

My Father, I have been "straining at the reins" . . . pulling hard to make certain things go my way . . . and irritated that you don't seem willing to work things my way.

Today, I hand the reins to you . . . I grant you all power. . . .

28
The Exchange

. . . consider yourselves dead to sin and alive to God. . . .

Romans 6:11, RSV

I have been crucified with Christ and I no longer live, but Christ lives in me.

Galatians 2:20

A cross Christian; an anxious, discouraged, or gloomy Christian; a doubting Christian; a selfish, cruel, or hardhearted Christian; a self-indulgent Christian; a Christian with a sharp tongue, or a bitter spirit:

In short, a Christian who is not Christlike may talk about his faith to the four winds—and he will have as much success as when he tries to tell his family and friends about Christ. His words will fall to the ground, dead, because those who are close to him see him as he really is.

There is no escape from the inevitable law of

things, and we may as well recognize it. If we want our loved ones to trust the Lord, volumes of talk about it will not be one-thousandth part as convincing to them as the sight of a little real trust on our own part when we're in need or crisis. The loudest prayer and the longest preaching are of no avail in any family circle—however convincing it may sound from a pulpit—unless the one who expounds the message lives out the very things he is preaching.

Some Christians think that the fruits which the Bible calls for are some form of outward religious work—such as holding more and more meetings, visiting the poor, conducting charitable works, and so forth. The Bible scarcely mentions these . . . but declares that the fruit of the Spirit is love, joy, peace, patience, kindness, goodness, faithfulness, gentleness and self-control (Galatians 5:22–23). A Christlike character must necessarily be the fruit of Christ's indwelling.

In order to become conformed to the image of Christ, we must of necessity be made "partakers of the divine nature" (2 Peter 1:4, KJV).

Our tastes, our wishes, our purposes will become like Christ's only when we change eyes with Him—when we begin to see things as He sees them. Then, a changed life will be inevitable.

GOD OF ALL COMFORT: Ch. 16

My Tender Father, show me the others in my world as you see them.

Show me if I've been irritable, or critical, just because I don't understand your dealings in their lives. And let me come over to your side, in how I treat them today.

29

A New Song of Victory

O sing to the Lord a new song, for he has done marvelous things! His right hand and his holy arm have gotten him victory.

———

Psalm 98:1, RSV

. . . and this is the victory that overcomes the world, our faith.

———

1 John 5:4, RSV

*H*undreds of times, I had read these words of our Savior: "I am the vine . . . apart from me you can do nothing" (John 15:5). But one day they were set ablaze for me with wondrous meaning—so much so that it seemed they must have been newly inserted into my Bible since last I had opened it. Here was our Lord, saying distinctly, "Without me, you can do nothing." And yet, all the while, I had been thinking I

131

could and must do so much.

What sort of meaning had I hitherto been giving to this word *nothing*? I tried to remember but all was a blank.

Another day, the same thing occurred as I read where our Lord tells us, "Do not worry about your life" (Matthew 6:25), on the ground that our heavenly Father concerns himself for us. . . . I read the passage over and over with utter amazement. Had it been in the Bible all these years? Why had I never seen it in so brilliant a light before?

In fact, I had known both these passages by heart. But in the only sense worth considering, I never had seen them before.

From that moment, every page of the Bible seemed to declare in trumpet tones the reality of a victorious life—but it must be lived by faith in the Lord Jesus Christ.

My whole soul was afire with my discovery. I had found out a "secret" about the salvation of Christ that I had never even dreamed, and it was this: He is a far more complete Savior than I had ever before imagined. I saw that He is not only my Savior for the future, but He is also my all-sufficient Savior for the present.

For it became him, for whom are all things, and by whom are all things, in bringing many sons unto glory, to make the captain of their salvation perfect through sufferings (Hebrews 2:10). He is my Burden-bearer, in order that I might roll the burdens off my own weak shoulders (Isaiah 53:4). He is my Fortress, to hide me from my enemies (Psalm 18:2) . . . my Shield, to protect me (Psalm 84:11) . . . my Guide, to lead me (Psalm 31:3) . . . my Comforter, to console me (John 14:26, KJV) . . . my Shepherd, to care for me (Psalm 23:1). . . .

I could not keep such wondrous news to myself.

THE UNSELFISHNESS OF GOD: Ch. 26

My Father, help me listen to my own words today—my "song of faith." Help me to notice what I say to others about the challenges spread before me.

Do I tell them, "I have such great problems"?

Or do I say, despite my problems, "I know a great God"?

30
No "Second Causes"

I am the Lord, and there is no other; apart from me there is no God. I will strengthen you, though you have not acknowledged me, so that from the rising of the sun to the place of its setting men may know there is none besides me. . . . I form the light and create darkness, I bring prosperity and create disaster; I, the Lord, do all these things."

Isaiah 45:5–7

Good and upright is the Lord. . . . All the ways of the Lord are loving and faithful. . . .

Psalm 25:8, 10

One of the greatest obstacles to an unwavering experience in the spiritual life is the difficulty of seeing God in everything.

People say, "I can easily submit to things that I know come from God—but I cannot submit to man, and most of my troubles come through other men and women!"

We know God cannot be the author of human failure, or ignorance, or carelessness, or sin—and yet, unless we trust Him to be our agent in the matter, how can we say to Him about it, "May your will be done"?

What is needed then is to see God in everything and to receive everything directly from His hands, with no intervention of "second causes." We need to take this step of faith, before we can ever know an abiding experience of peaceful, joyful abandonment, and the rest that comes from perfect trust. Remember: Our abandonment is to God and not to man.

To the children of God, everything comes directly from their Father's hands without regard to the "second cause" that brings it about. . . . The whole teaching of Scripture asserts and implies this:

Not a sparrow falls to the ground apart from the will of your Father (Matthew 10:29).

The very hairs of your head are numbered (v.30).

We are not to take revenge on anyone ourselves, because our heavenly Father has charged himself with our defense (Romans 12:19).

No one can be against us, for He is for us (Romans 8:31).

We shall not want, for He is our Shepherd (Psalm 23:1).

He shall give His angels charge over you, to keep you in all your ways (Psalm 91:11) . . .

So that we may boldly say, "The Lord is my helper, and I will not fear what man may do to me" (Hebrews 13:6).

To my own mind these Scriptures and many others like them, settle forever the question of the power behind "second causes" in the life of the children of God. Second causes must all be under the control of our Father, and not one of them can touch us except with His knowledge . . . nothing can disturb or harm us except He shall see that it is best for us and shall stand aside to let it pass.

I learned this lesson practically, and in my own experience, long before I discovered that there is actually a scriptural principle here.

I was attending a prayer meeting . . . when a lady I did not recognize stood to speak. . . . She confessed she'd had great difficulty in living the life of faith, because it seemed that "second causes"—in fact, everything and everyone but God—seemed to control almost every aspect of her life. Her trouble and confusion became so intense that she began to ask God to teach her whether He really was in everything or not.

After praying this way for days, this came to her as in a vision:

She was in a perfectly dark place, and there came toward her from a distance, a body of light which gradually surrounded and enveloped her and everything around her. As it was approaching, a voice seemed to say, "This is the presence of God!"

While surrounded with this wonderful presence, all the great and awful things of life seemed to pass before her—fighting armies, wicked men, raging beasts, storms and diseases, sin and suffering of every kind. She shrank back at first in terror—but soon she saw that the presence of God so surrounded and enveloped her and each one of these things that not a lion could reach out its paw, nor a bullet fly through the air, except as the Presence of God moved out of the way to permit it.

She also saw that, if there were ever so thin a film, as it were, of this glorious Presence between herself and the most terrible violence, not a hair of her head could be ruffled, nor anything touch her, except as the Presence divided and let the evil through.

Then all the small and annoying things of life passed before her, and she saw that . . . not a cross look, nor a harsh word, nor petty trial of any kind could affect her unless God's encircling Presence moved out of the way to let it.

Nothing else but this—seeing God in everything—will make us loving and patient. . . . Nothing else will completely put an end to the murmuring and rebelling thoughts.

The human beings around us are often the "bottles" that hold our spiritual medicine, but it is our Father's hand of love that pours out the medicine. . . . The human bottle is the "second cause" and has no real agency in itself. For the medicine these human bottles hold is prescribed for us and given to us by the Great Physician of our souls.

THE CHRISTIAN'S SECRET OF A HAPPY LIFE: Ch. 12

My Physician Father, I see it now. . . .

For every one of my soul-sicknesses, you give me a "medicine" for my healing.

For my pride and independence, you give one who likes to dominate. For my impatience, you send one who grates. For my criticalness, you give me one who is sorry indeed.

Today, I will receive your treatments . . . even if they sting.

31
Stillness

Be still, and know that I am God."

Psalm 46:10

*T*he Israelites of old, like many Christians today, could not believe that *quietness* and *rest* were the way to deliverance and strength. As they struggled, so we struggle to deliver ourselves by earthly means and creaturely activities.

It was as useless for them as it is for us.

The truth is, the way of inner stillness is the only victorious way. . . . To settle down and know this as fact would immensely change us. . . . Only when we first stand still can we see the salvation of our Lord. While full of bustle and activity, we have no eyes to spare for God's work. Moreover, our feverish, creaturely workings—far from helping—actually hinder His true work.

To many, this seems like pure laziness. They may think that nothing can be accomplished under such conditions. But we are only to sit still because God works. . . . The Lord cannot rest while there remains anything unfinished for His people, as no good earthly parent can rest as long as a child is in need.

To "sit still" in our hearts means to learn and to practice inner stillness. It may mean an outward stillness as well . . . or it may be accompanied with great outward activity—though never with jostling and anxious hurry.

Then, let there be storms of hail outside. Within, the "home" that is created for the spirit is a quiet resting place in God.

EVERYDAY RELIGION: Ch. 17

My Father, I will "help along" your working in my life today . . . by practicing stillness within.

32

The "Order" of Love

This is love: not that we loved God. . . . We love [him] because he first loved us.

1 John 4:10, 19

I must tell thee a splendid idea of God I got from thy sad account of the Countess. Thee said she found [her husband, the Count] intolerable "not from anything he actually does or does not do, but just simply from what he is."

Now I had been chafing over some religious expressions, such as, "The cross of Christ is the source and cause of our love for Christ," and similar sentiments based on things He did for us. They seemed to me utterly inadequate somehow.

To die on the cross was nothing to Him. In fact, if it was to help His creatures God could *not* want not to. . . .

But as I read thy letter about Count, it came to me in a flash. Of course we never love people for what they do or don't do. We love them or hate them for what they are, for the personality that is behind the action and that makes the action possible.

I love God because He is lovable, and for no other reason whatever. I may find out by His doings that He is lovable, but His doings are of no other account as a factor in my loving. "We love Him because He first loved us"—I had a lovely time in my wakeful hours last night thinking of this.

We love Him, not because of a single thing He does or does not do, but just because He first loved us. . . .

I believe the real question that ought to be put to the soul is not "Do you love God?" but "Do you believe God is lovable?"

UNPUBLISHED LETTER: May 2, 1910

My Father, I know that you cannot help but love . . . because you are Love.

May it be, today, that I understand how lovable you are . . . so that my spirit may overflow with love to all . . . even those whose touch is hard.

33
The Unselfishness of God

Philip said [to Jesus], "Lord, show us the Father, and that will be enough for us."

John 14:8

God is Light and in him is no darkness at all . . . if we are living in the light of God's presence, just as Christ does, then we have wonderful fellowship and joy . . . and the blood of Jesus his Son cleanses us. . . .

1 John 1:5–7, TLB

If I were called upon to state in one sentence the sum and substance of my spiritual experience, it is this: Each one of us must rediscover the unselfishness of God.

To know God as He really is, in His essential nature and character, is to have reached the absolute and unchangeable, the utterly satisfying foundation, upon which we can then rear the whole superstructure of our spiritual life.

If you want to know the answer to every human question, the cure for every human ill, it lies here: to discover that God is not the selfish Being we are so apt to think of Him, but is instead fundamentally unselfish. He cares not at all for himself, but only and always for our welfare.

How to make this discovery is the crucial question. In our present stage of existence we have not the faculties to actually see God in His incomprehensible Being. We need an Interpreter.

To know God as He really is, we must look to His incarnation in the Lord Jesus Christ. . . . When one of the disciples said to Christ, "Show us the Father, and that will be enough," Jesus answered, "Don't you know me . . . even after I have been among you such a long time? Anyone who has seen me has seen the Father" (John 14:8–9).

Here then is our opportunity. We cannot see God, but we can see Christ. . . . Whatever Christ was, God is. All the unselfishness, tenderness, kindness, justice, goodness—all that and more— we see in Christ, and it is nothing more or less than a revelation of God our Father, as He longs for us to know Him.

By discovering God, therefore, I do not mean something mysterious, or mystical, or something that cannot be attained by the ordinary man or woman. . . . I simply mean finding out what sort of Being He really is, whether good or bad, kind or unkind, strong or weak, wise or foolish, just or unjust.

Everything in your spiritual life depends on the sort of God you worship. Because the character of the worshiper will always be molded by the character of what He worships: If it is a cruel and revengeful God, the worshiper will be the same, but if it is a loving, tender, forgiving, unselfish God, the worshiper will be transformed slowly, wonderfully, into this likeness.

This makes all the difference in our practical, earthly lives as well. For once we glimpse the real God, as He is revealed in Jesus Christ, from that moment our peace flows like an unstoppable river. And through everything that happens to us, even at times when we can rejoice in nothing else—we will be able to "rejoice in the God of our salvation."

Then we no longer need even His promises, bountiful as they are, for we have found God himself. And He is all that we need.

THE UNSELFISHNESS OF GOD: Introduction

My Unselfish Father, I set aside all asking . . . all my needs and requests of you. Today . . . just now . . . I want only you.

34
One Law

*Let no debt remain outstanding, except the
continuing debt to love one another, for he who loves
his fellowman has fulfilled the law.*

Romans 13:8

There is one spiritual law that is, in itself, the
fulfillment of all other laws.

The Apostle Paul writes:

"The entire law is summed up in a single
command: 'Love your neighbor as yourself' "
(Galatians 5:14).

"Love does no harm to its neighbor. Therefore
love is the fulfillment of the law" (Romans 13:10).

It is the very nature of love that it cannot harm
its neighbor, knowing that to do so is always evil.
It is as impossible for love to harm, as it is for the
sun to produce darkness instead of light.

We must remember, however, that a great deal
of what is called love ought really to be spelled
s-e-l-f-i-s-h-n-e-s-s.

People love their own enjoyment of their

friends more than they love the friends. People consider their own well-being, over and above the well-being of those they say they love.

We never really love someone until we can do without them, if our doing without them will result in their own good. Measured by this test— do you really love?

Love can never mean cherishing yourself at the expense of another.

EVERYDAY RELIGION: Ch. 15

My Father, *today I call upon you to be the gentle judge of my innermost heart.*

Let your truth shine into me. . . . Do I care for someone, only because they do what is good for me? How do I react when their will crosses mine?

35
The Divine Rule of Faith

*T*his is the assurance we have in approaching God,
that if we ask anything according to his will, he hears
us. And if we know that he hears us—whatever we
ask—we know that we have what we asked of him.

———

1 John 5:14–15

*[T*he Lord] said to me, "My grace is sufficient for
you, for my power is made perfect in weakness."

———

2 Corinthians 12:9

*F*aith is the conquering rule of the universe.

God spoke, and it was done. Relying on Him,
we too may speak, and it shall be done.

A wonderful light streamed upon the
promise, written by the Apostle John—"we know
that we have what we ask of him." I had always
thought of this passage as one of the beautiful
dreams of the Christian life that nobody, in their

right senses, supposed for a moment was meant to be realized in this world.

Then I saw it was no dream, but simply a statement of divine law—the law of faith, as certain in its action as the law of gravity, if only one understood it.

Our Lord tells us over and over that according to our faith it shall be unto us. He actually asserts, without any limitations, that "everything is possible for him who believes" (Mark 9:23). But I had never supposed this was anything more than a romance.

Not at all. He was stating a law of the spiritual kingdom we must enter, a law which anyone can try and prove for himself.

Faith links us to the almighty power of God, and makes it possible for our weakness to draw down unfailing supplies of His strength, poured on us out of His love—and when I first saw this there seemed no limit to its possibilities.

Faith, mighty faith, the promise sees
    and looks at that alone.
Faith laughs at impossibilities
    and says, "It shall be done!"

I wish I could say that I have always, since then, lived in the power of this divine law of faith. But one thing I can say, that whenever I have chosen to lay hold of God's strength by faith it has always been made perfect in my weakness.

In this way, I have had victory. Over and over,

I have been able to say with the apostle, "In [everything] we are more than conquerors through him who loved us" (Romans 8:37).

THE UNSELFISHNESS OF GOD: Ch. 26

My Faithful Father, at times I have looked for some great blast of power to fall from heaven, scattering all my enemies and fears . . . have wanted answers more than the grace of knowing you.

Now I hear the spirit-wind snapping your victory flag over me—the banner that says, "Love." And it comes clear that, as I travel under this banner, my soul remains safe from worldly traps.

36
On Believing

*Jesus humbled himself and became obedient to death—
even death on a cross! Therefore God exalted him to
the highest place and gave him the name that is above
every name, that at the name of Jesus every knee
should bow, in heaven and on earth and under the
earth. . . .*

Philippians 2:8–10

*Jesus asked them, "Do you believe that I am able to do
this?"*

Matthew 9:28

Thou ask about my personal faith. . . . I give
to thee my confession. . . .

I believe in God the Father, and in God the
Son, and God the Holy Spirit—one God, with
different means of showing himself.

I believe God loves the creatures He has
created and that, being a just God, His will is to
make us good. And though the Devil may work

155

all manner of evil against us—whether it come in the guise of illness, or lack, or wounds from a friend—he shall not, cannot prevail!

I believe that in order to accomplish so great a salvation, God came to be a man and to die for us. And on this next point I know that I differ from those who loudly insist on their own "orthodoxy," and must continue to differ, because to me their views are God-dishonoring. For I have come to know of a certainty that doctrine alone, without the Spirit, can become one of Satan's most wicked and cruel instruments, can actually be used as libel against our God who is love (1 John 4:8).

And this is the strong point on which I have founded myself: God did not die for us merely to appease himself, but to appease our consciences and to make us know His love.

I believe the atonement means at-one-ment. I believe that the separation was all on our side, not on His. I believe that the whole world is already forgiven (see John 3:16–17), and that all each one of us needs to do is to find this out as fact, and to believe it.

I believe God has revealed himself to us as our Brother as well as our Savior in the Lord Jesus Christ (Romans 8:29), and that His appearing was a first glimpse, a demonstration, of how much He intends for us to be made at-one with Him. So to me, Christ is a personal Savior . . . as God himself, pouring out His yearning love and pity (Isaiah 63:8–9).

Knowing all this, I rest in the love of God. Therefore, I can also rejoice in His will, whatever it may be. And so I have no anxieties about anything in heaven or on earth. Because of this, I am satisfied with my allotment in every particular, because I see it all as the will of my God. I have so completely handed over the care of myself into His hands that I have no further concern about myself.

And now I must ask of thee, dear friend: Are thou willing to be anything it pleases Him to make thee?

UNPUBLISHED LETTER: September 23, 1876

My Father, I come to you now . . . to lay all that weighs on me, all that drives me, in your open hands.

And in those hands I see the imprinted scars . . . and know that you are completely, only, worthy to be trusted.

37

The Comforter Is Come

And I will pray the Father, and he shall give you another Comforter, that he may abide with you forever. . . . I will not leave you comfortless: I will come to you.

John 14:16, 18, KJV

. . . everything else is worthless when compared with the priceless gain of knowing Christ Jesus my Lord. I have put aside all else, counting it worth less than nothing, in order that I can have Christ, and become one with him. . . .

Philippians 3:8–9, TLB

Our Comforter is not far off in heaven, where we cannot find Him. He is close at hand. He always lives with us, in us.

The very words "abiding Comforter" are an amazing revelation of God. Meditate on them, until you comprehend what they mean! If we can have a friend to stay with us and comfort us for even a few days when we are facing some trouble, we feel fortunate. But here is the promise of a heavenly Comforter who is here now, always staying with us, and whose power is infinite.

But the uneasy soul will ask whether this divine Comforter does not sometimes reprove us for our sins. And how can there be any comfort in that?

In my opinion, that is exactly one of the places where the comfort is most needed to come in. For what sort of people would we be if we had no divine Teacher always at hand to show us when we are wandering in a wilderness of faults and awaken in us a desire to get rid of them?

If I am walking along the street with an embarrassing tear in the back of my dress, and I do not know it is there, it is a comfort to have a good friend who is kind enough to tell me about it. Similarly, it is indeed wonderful to know that there is, with me always, a divine, all-seeing Comforter, who will correct me in my faults and will not simply allow me to go on in fatal unconsciousness of them. . . . The Lord restores comfort to us by revealing our sin, and healing it (see Isaiah 57:16–18).

The path to finding the comforting of God lies in seeing our weaknesses, sins and needs. This explains to me better than anything else the reason why the Lord so often allows sorrow and trial to come our way.

"Therefore, behold, I will allure [you], and bring [you] into the wilderness, and speak comfortably unto [you]" (Hosea 2:14, KJV).

We find ourselves, perhaps, in a "wilderness" of disappointment or of suffering, and we wonder why the God who loves us should have allowed it. But He knows that it is only in this very wilderness that we can hear and receive the comforting words He wants to pour upon us. We must feel the need of comfort before we can listen to the words.

In His way of consoling, God will always give us a far better thing than what we have lost. The things we lose, precious to us as they are, are earthly things: He replaces them with heavenly things.

If God were to "lure" you into an earthly wilderness, would you not thankfully go through any difficulty to get there, knowing your journey would end with you finding the unspeakable joy of union with Him? Paul said he "considered everything a loss" for the goal of "gaining Christ." If we have even the slightest glimpse of what it means to "gain Christ," we will say so, too.

My Father, show me what passing earthly goal I can turn from pursuing today . . .

. . . so that I can take hold of another piece of eternity, in knowing you.

38
In God Alone

. . . rejoice in the Lord!

———

Philippians 3:1

*Singers and dancers alike say, "All my springs [of
joy] are in you."*

———

Psalm 87:7, RSV

*But let all who take refuge in you be glad; let them
ever sing for joy. . . .*

———

Psalm 5:11

*T*he consummation of all Christian
experience—the place where our soul is finally
enfolded in the Spirit of God—is this: when we
learn to rejoice in the Lord and to be satisfied
with Him alone!

In our moments of spiritual exaltation we
sometimes seem (to ourselves) to have climbed
our way to great wisdom, great strength, or other

spiritual riches in which to glory. But then we come down from the mountaintop into the humdrum routine of daily life, and these grand spiritual possessions all disappear. We are left with nothing to glory in.

Even what we call "spiritual blessings" and "spiritual gifts" are full of the element of change. The prayer which is answered today may seem to be unanswered tomorrow. The promises once so gloriously fulfilled may abruptly cease to have any apparent fulfillment. The spiritual blessing which was at one time such a joy may be utterly lost. And nothing of all that we once trusted in, rested our souls upon, may be left to us—nothing but hunger, emptiness and longing.

But when all else is gone, God is still left. . . . He is the same yesterday, today and forever (Hebrews 13:8), and in Him there is no "variableness" for He does not change like shifting shadows (James 1:17, KJV).

The only lasting joy is to be found in the everlasting God . . . apart from all else—apart from His gifts, apart from His blessings.

He is always the same good, loving, tender God. . . . Of Him we can say, "You have made known to me the path of life; you will fill me with joy in your presence, with eternal pleasures at your right hand" (Psalm 16:11).

To the children of God there stands, behind all that changes and can change, only one unchangeable joy. That is God. . . .

Neglect, indifference, forgetfulness, ignorance are all impossible to Him. And He knows everything about us. And He cares about everything. Moreover, He can manage every situation. And He loves us!

Surely this is enough to open the wellsprings of joy. . . . And joy is always a source of strength.

EVERYDAY RELIGION: Ch. 8

My Father, I have felt my soul turning toward you . . . only to feel the world calling me back, whispering that I am being a fool. . . .

Beyond all spiritual feelings . . . beyond all wonderful gifts . . . seize me with a true knowledge of this . . . just that you are.

39
Yes

Jesus said . . . "My prayer is . . . that . . . [they may] be in us so that the world may believe that you have sent me . . . that they may be one as we are one: I in them and you in me."

John 17:1, 20–23

All the dealings of God with the soul of the believer are in order to bring it into oneness with himself, that this prayer of Jesus may be fulfilled.

This divine union was the glorious purpose in the heart of God for His people before the foundations of the world. It was the mystery hid from ages and generations. It was accomplished in the death of Christ. It has been made known by the Scriptures. And it is realized as an actual experience by many of God's children.

But not by all.

God has not hidden it or made it hard, but the eyes of many are too dim to the spiritual world, and so their hearts are too unbelieving for them to grasp this idea of oneness. It is for the purpose

167

of bringing us into oneness that the Lord calls us so earnestly and so repeatedly to abandon ourselves to Him. And only in this way may He work in us all the good pleasure of His will.

All the previous steps in the Christian life lead to the head of this very path: our journey toward oneness with God.

The Lord has made this way for us. And until we understand the way clearly, and have voluntarily consented to embrace it, the cry of God's own Spirit for us will not be satisfied. Nor will our hearts find their destined and real rest.

This spiritual union is not a matter of emotions, but of growing in the character of Christ. It is not something we are to feel, but something we are to be. True, we may feel it very blessedly, and probably shall; the vital thing, however, is not to found your faith on feelings but on the reality.

To the natural, darkened, unbelieving mind with which each one of us is born, it seems too wonderful to be true that we should be created for such a high purpose as this. And yet it is a blessed reality. . . . Do you understand the words, "one with Christ"? Do you catch the slightest glimpse of their marvelous meaning? Does not your whole soul begin to exult. . . ?

We are commanded to enter into such a life. We are exhorted to lay down our own lives that His life may be lived in us. We are asked to have no interests but His interests—to share His riches, to enter into His joys, to partake of His sorrows, to show others His likeness, to have the same mind He had, to think and feel and act and walk as He did.

Will you consent to all this? The Lord will not force it on you, for He wants you as His companion and His friend.

Will you say a willing yes to your Lord?

THE CHRISTIAN'S SECRET OF A HAPPY LIFE: Ch. 19

My loving, generous, gentle
Father . . .

. . . yes. . . .

40
God Is Enough

You hem me in—behind and before; you have laid
your hand upon me. . . . Where can I go from your
Spirit? Where can I flee from your presence? If I go up
to the heavens, you are there; if I make my bed in the
depths . . . even there your hand will guide me. . . .
All the days ordained for me were written in your
book before one of them came to be.

Psalm 139:5, 7–8, 10, 16

. . . the light of your face [shines] upon us, O Lord.
You have filled my heart with greater joy than when
grain and new wine abound . . . for you alone . . .
make me dwell in safety.

Psalm 4:6–8

As long as our attention is turned upon
ourselves and our own experiences—whether
good or bad—then our face is turned away from
the Lord. Do you see that this is plain common
sense?

While we are looking at ourselves, we can never "see God." It is not that He hides himself; He is always there in full view of all who look unto Him. But we will not see Him as long as we look in any other direction.

It may be that, until now, our eyes have been so exclusively fixed upon ourselves that all our inner questioning has captured all our attention: Is my love for God "warm" enough? Is my faith fervent enough? Do I feel my sins painfully enough . . . desire the things I need earnestly enough?

If we want to continue in our journey, if we want to see God, then we must stop endlessly questioning about ourselves, and focus all our questions on Him: How does God feel toward me? Is His love for me warm enough? Has He done enough to accomplish my salvation? Does He feel every one of my daily needs enough?

Do I need to supply the answer to these questions? . . . Let our needs and difficulties be as great as they may, there is for all our needs a supply of love and grace and strength that is immeasurably more than we can ask or imagine (see Ephesians 3:20).

Just because He is, just because we are His, all must go right for us.

God's saints through all ages have known . . . that God was enough for them. . . . Nothing can separate you from His love, absolutely nothing—neither death nor life, nor angels nor principalities nor powers, nor things present nor things to come, nor height nor depth, nor any malevolent creature. . . .

You can, you must settle this fact once and for all: God, who is love—who is, if I may say it this way, made out of love—simply cannot help but shed blessing on blessing upon us. We do not need to beg, for He simply cannot help it!

God is enough for time, and for all time.

God is enough for eternity.

God is enough!

GOD OF ALL COMFORT: Ch. 17

My heart is the wandering compass needle . . . but you are my magnetic north . . . O my Father! My true home!

I will set my face to follow you today, and every day to come, journeying toward the higher hills of faith. How I long to meet you there face to face!

And I know that, no matter what may rise to hinder me, you will be with me all the way . . . to keep me safe within your love.

DAVID HAZARD developed the "Rekindling the Inner Fire" devotional series to encourage others to keep the "heart" of their faith alive and afire with love for God. He also feels a special need to help Christians of today to "meet" men and women of the past whose experience of God belongs to the whole Church, for all the ages.

Hazard is an award-winning writer, the author of books for both adults and children, with international bestsellers among his many titles. He lives in northern Virginia with his wife, MaryLynne, and three children: Aaron, Joel, and Sarah Beth.